A

A MINNESOTA REMEMBRANCE
Making A Life In The Land God Forgot

Robert O. Harde

Cover Design by Allison Souter

The Niels Nielsen homestead on south sho
(L to R) Fred Nelson, Martin Tingdale holding baby Mildred, Josie Nielsen Ting

on Lake near Tamarack, Minnesota circa 1900.
rus Nelson, Mrs. & Mrs. Niels Nielsen, unidentified. Note the cup in the window.

Please direct all correspondence and book orders to:
Jerry Rosnau
Director
Aitkin County Historical Society
P.O. Box 215
Aitkin, MN 56431

ISBN 0-9665976-0-5

Published by the Aitkin County Historical Society

Printed in the United States of America

PREFACE TO THE SERIES

This book of letters, photographs, and illustrations is the first in a series about the lives of the Marcus Nelson family - my grandparents, mother and uncle - and, by extension, the story of many other Aitkin County, Minnesota pioneer settlers. Of the number of ways to describe a study of this nature, I chose to call it a remembrance. For at its core, it is both a record of memories past and a memento of those times; a gift from the ages, if you will, to all the generations that come after mine - the last living link to these pioneers.

I want to emphasize this body of work is not a textbook written by some pipe-smoking professor. Nay, this is a story told by real people of the time, recorded with their own pens, cameras, and drawings. Throughout this series, it is they who will tell and show what the north country was truly like during the period 1892 to 1938. For unlike most historical treatments that look down though time and describe events in distant, bloodless tones, these volumes allow you the reader the opportunity to get up close and personal with the Nelsons - to, in fact, share their lives vicariously. The Nelsons shortcomings and strengths, accomplishments and disappointment, joys and rage, blessings and tragedy, become yours as well.

Why a book about somebody you never heard of? The answer begins with the staggering amount of visual and written documentation available about the Marcus Nelsons. This is rare, particularly in a non-prominent family. The first part of the why, then, is that it could be done. But that alone would not justify this undertaking. What makes the story of unknown people interesting and important is when it make a connection with you, when it provides a context for your own place in the world. Such a narrative serves as a time machine - revealing things long forgotten or previously unknown about your own grandparents, great-uncles and aunts, great-grandparents, and so on. It is, then, this commonality with the many, this intimate touching of the past, this personal unwillingness to sever the Nelson's life continuum, that has caused me to bring their story to light.

In this first volume, Marcus and his Norwegian family have taken up a homestead in Aitkin County, one-hundred and thirty miles north of Minneapolis and St. Paul. Notwithstanding the pronouncements in Chicago of historian Frederick Jackson Turner, this region was still a raw frontier in 1892. During the 1890's, the extended Nielsen family somehow manages to eke a living from out of "the land that God forgot," an expression occasionally used by the settlers when they realized how hard farming was in a region of harsh climate, forest fires, poor soil, and remote location. (While dairying was important for a long time, potatoes were the only meaningful cash crop the ground ever yielded). Yet, while the land is not particularly kind to the farmer, it smiles on Marcus. During the first decade of the new century, he grows to a strapping manhood, marries Mamie Barnett, starts a family, and enjoys a flowering business career.

Future volumes will further explore Marcus' pursuits in logging and storekeeping, the commonplace of disease, accident, and death, the great forest fire of 1918, the children's coming of age in Minneapolis during the Roaring Twenties, the shattering effects of bankruptcy and near poverty, Marcus' political career, his daughter's adventures in teaching and brushes with romance, a daring 1924 automobile trip to the Yellowstone, and the extraordinary aviation career of his son.

This work would not be in your hands without my grandmother's strong sense of family history and lifelong habit of drawing and painting, taking and saving photographs, preserving letters and diaries, and, late in life, the creation of personal memoirs. Her fanaticism even extended to requesting (and usually getting) the return of great numbers of letters she had written to others! Mamie Nelson also wrote or inspired several regional histories about Aitkin County's early settlers. It is her legacy, and the other sources noted in the bibliography, that enabled me to tell this story accurately and in authentic "voice."

Some housekeeping items. Fractured syntax and spelling inconsistencies were a matter of course for these folks. I retained their manner of written expression whenever practical because so much meaning and originality (to say nothing of the humor!) would have been lost using modern standard English. Still, due to repetition, ambiguities, illegibility, and the other confusing elements that invariably appear in any large body of correspondence, virtually all the letters required some degree of editing and rewriting. Nevertheless, I wish to make clear that, except for a few minor dramatic compressions and the clarifications provided in the End Notes, all the people and events portrayed are real and true.

Finally, this volume (and those to come) has many authors. While some of the letters presented were created by me from secondary sources, the large majority are derived from genuine letters, combinations of letters, or other documents written by the persons to whom I have attributed them. I would be pleased if the reader made the assumption that the better portions of this work flowed from their hand.

Robert O. Harder
May 11, 1998
Chicago, Illinois

Schoolcraft's map of 1820.

Sandy Lake is shown larger than Spirit Lake (Mille Lacs), a reflection of its importance in the fur trade.

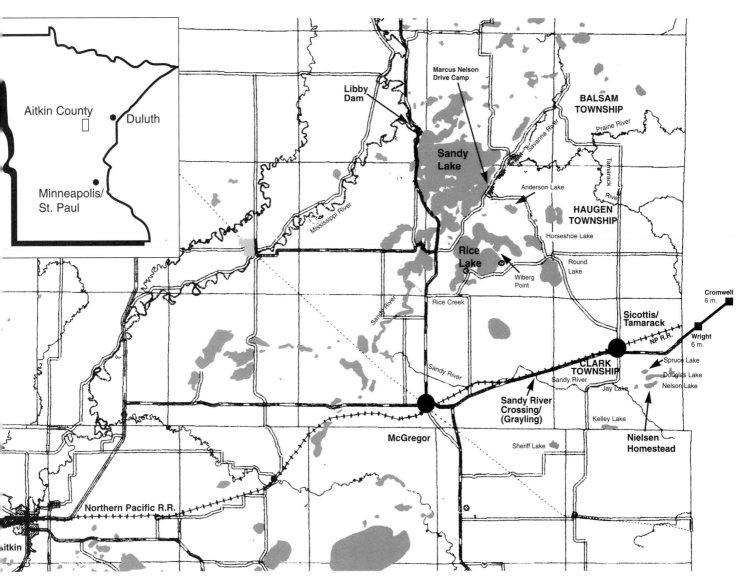

Eastern Aitkin County at the turn of the century.

Aitkin County
Duluth

Minneapolis/
St. Paul

Libby
Dam

Marcus Nelson
Drive Camp

BALSAM
TOWNSHIP

Sandy
Lake

Prairie River

Savanna River

Anderson Lake

Tamarack River

HAUGEN
TOWNSHIP

Mississippi River

Horseshoe Lake

Rice
Lake

Round
Lake

Wiberg
Point

Cromwell
6 m.

Rice Creek

Sicottis/
Tamarack

NP R.R.

Wright
6 m.

Sandy River

CLARK
TOWNSHIP

Spruce Lake

Douglas Lake

Sandy River

Nelson Lake

Jay Lake

Sandy River
Crossing/
(Grayling)

Kelley Lake

McGregor

Nielsen
Homestead

Sheriff Lake

Northern Pacific R.R.

itkin

PART ONE

The Niels Nielsen family in Grimstad, Norway, Circa 1880.
Front (L to R): Josie, Anna holding Marcus, Christine, Martha.
Back (L to R): Ole, Emma, Fred.

H

By 1880, steamboats had generally replaced sailing vessels and demand for wood figureheads and rigging pulleys in the Smith-Petersen shipyards of Grimstad, Norway plummeted. Niels Nielsen, a talented and moderately well off Billedhogger (sculptor or carver), found himself short on opportunity. With wife Anna, children Marcus, Frederick, Ole, Josephine, Ingeborg (Emma), Christine, and Martha, he immigrated to Chicago. In 1885 the family moved to Minneapolis, scraping together odd jobs for another seven years. In 1892, Niels, Fred, and thirteen-year-old Marcus boarded a train for northern Minnesota. Their destination was a tiny Northern Pacific railroad siding called Sicottis, where nearby the family had taken up a one hundred sixty acre homestead. On that September day, the Niels Nielsens became the first full-blood white family to settle in what became Clark Township, Aitkin County, Minnesota.

Niels Nielsen carving wood figureheads for sailing ships. Circa 1870s.

The Smith-Petersen Boat Works.

Grimstad seen from sea side. Arrow p

FREDK SMITH PETERSEN
GRIMSTAD

At the request of Niels Nielsen, joiner and carver in wood, turner, and blockmaker, I hereby beg to certify, that the said Nielsen, after having been in my employment as blockmaker at my building yard, has successively carved the ornaments and figure heads for all the vessels I have built since 1868 viz. thirteen. Mr. Nielsen has distinguished himself for an exquisite good taste, he is an assiduous worker, and his invention of new patterns is a proof of his natural talent. For my own part I deplore that he has decided to emigrate to America, as it will now be impossible to get our ships so tastefully carved and ornamented.

Grimstad, 12th July 1880   (signed)

Fredk Smith Petersen

Ship Owner & Builder

Grimstad and

...ouse where Niels Nielsen family lived.

The undersigned consul of the German Empire at this port do hereby certify the above to be in the handwriting of and signed by Mr. Fredrik Smith Petersen, Ship Owner and Builder of this town. From my own experience I also know Mr. Nielsen is a highly respectable and worthy man, whose workmanship has won him a name on this southern coast of Norway.

Grimstad at the Vice-Consulate
of the German Empire
12th July 1880

(signed)
[signature illegible]
Viceconsul

...rom land side.

Bill Sicottis' 1873 trading post and locomotive wood station and water tank.

Settlers arriving at the Tamarack Northern Pacific Railroad Depot. Section house to left.

Minneapolis
Sept 14, 1892

Dear Bror Marcus,

    Pa's letter said you come in on the Northern Pacific P.M train and spent the night at what he called the "littil merwin shak" as it was the only other building in sight beside the section house. Said not all your stuff made it when changed trains at Carlton. Leastways that's what I think he said. He ought to stop mixing languages. Did you talk to the N.P. section foreman there - name of Gunderson I believe - about the missing goods?

    Now Marcus, what is this about the trip out to our claim? What in Creation could you have been thinking when Pa got dry and then lost when he went looking for a drink over to Sandy River. The next time you hear a man halloing for help in the brush, you hallo back and help him out of his fix instead of sitting on a rock laughing like a dumb cluck. That Mr. Clark, the hunter from down the way, was right in giving you a talking to. You know good and well Pa is a city man and needs looking after. We expect you at least to keep your head on the right end.

    Is the lien-to up yet? Can you not get help to cut logs for the house? Did Fred make it to the haying camp? Watch over Pa and yourself as it will do little good if you take sick.

    We are tolerable well here. It's hard at the iron works but the pay is steady and we are building on our pile. You make sure the house gets up.

    Your bror, Ole Nielsen

P.S. How is Jack the Dog?

Mpls
Sept 20, 1892

My Dear Marcus,

    This is your sister-in-law writing for your Ma. She got a letter from Pa where he told about the shooting and said it scared him about sick. Said the gun fell off the wheelbarrow and went off and tore a hole in your pants the size of a fist.

    Fred wrote he will stay to Sandy River Crossing until they finish making Dick Reed's slough hay. Money is scarce and Reed pays all right, thirty-five cents a day plus bed & board. Fred is to go to the claim soons he's done.

    You ought to be grateful to your neighbors Jay Clark and John Maxwell for getting hold of a team of oxen to drag out the heavy goods. Did they charge any?

    Ole shipped more of our stuff so be on the lookout. Pa says your lien-to is fit to store in and we got no place to keep things in this awful building. Would have to let it go for nothing so better to chance spoiling it.

    Now take time to hunt up some real food. Pa will eat nothing but cheese and crackers if you let him. How is it you have no plates, spoons, or forks? Were they lost at Carlton?

    Ma misses you boys terribly. Ole is laid up in bed with a sour belly from something he et. He is calling for me so I better hike. G'nite.

    Mrs. Ole Nielsen

Mr. & Mrs. Ole Nielsen

Marcus Nielsen and Jay Clark (r)   *Fred Nielsen*

STATE OF MINNESOTA, ss.
COUNTY OF HENNEPIN.

DISTRICT COURT.
FOURTH JUDICIAL DISTRICT.

I, *Niels Nielsen* do hereby, upon my oath declare that I first arrived in the United States on or about the _17_ day of _Aug_ in the year A. D. _1880_ and that I have, ever since that time, continued to reside in the United States, and that it is bona fide my intention to become **A CITIZEN OF THE UNITED STATES,** and to renounce forever all allegiance and fidelity which I in any wise owe to any foreign Prince, Potentate, State or Sovereignty; and particularly all allegiance and fidelity which I owe to the *King of Sweden & Norway* of whom I have heretofore been a subject.

Niels Nielson

Subscribed and sworn to before me this _____ day of _____ A. D. 188_

O E Dickey
Deputy Clerk of said Court.

STATE OF MINNESOTA, ss.
COUNTY OF HENNEPIN.

DISTRICT COURT.
FOURTH JUDICIAL DISTRICT.

I HEREBY CERTIFY That the foregoing is a true copy of the original declaration of *Niels Nielson* ____ this day filed in my office.

IN TESTIMONY WHEREOF I have hereunto set my hand and affixed the seal of said Court, at Minneapolis, in the County aforesaid, the _____ day of _____ A. D. 188_

E J Davenport
Clerk of said Court.

O E Dickey
Deputy.

Declaration of Intention dated 1886.

we have to do is sit on the place every now and then.

The legal description of our claim is: "The North half of the North East quarter, the South West quarter of the North East quarter and the North East quarter of the North West quarter of Section twenty-six in Township forty-eight North, of Range twenty-two West of the Fourth Principal Meridian in Minnesota, containing one hundred and sixty acres." In plain English, it's on the south shore of what they call Bass Lake, some three miles by crow southeast of whatever the name of that siding is. Fred wrote the N.P. calls it Tamarack Siding on account all that bog land used to be filled up with tamarack trees that got cut into firewood for the locomotives. But the little bitty dot on map says Sicottis. Guess it don't matter either way.

Ole

Mpls
September 25, '92

Bror Marcus,

Pa has gone off the beam about the way the homestead works. He don't need to be a citizen as he has filed a Declaration of Intention to do same. It is with his other papers in the box. The U.S. bets us a quarter section of their land that we can't last on it for five years. You got to pay a $10 filing fee, which we did, build a house on the land, and make certain improvements over the years. If we do all this we prove up and get the deed to the property. Get that notion out of Pa's head that all

Sandy River Crossing
Sept. 30, 1892

Brother Marcus,

Jay Clark and John Maxwell stopped by on there way back from a hunt. They whore black deerskin clothes and carried big rifles. Jay smokes them black for waterproveing. Somebody said John Maxwell is mostly Injun but you would not know to look at him. They both were brown as berries and as natural as old shoes.

Dick Reed is happy with the hay crop but it dont look much account to me. It is so late in the year the stuff we are pressing now has turned to wire. The N.P. cars loading up are headed for Dak. where they are hard up for fodder.

Ole wrote he dont think you fellows are eating right. Theres pike in the lake set some nets over by that crik on the north side. Geese mallards and teel are thick here and must be there too. Get up afore dawn and sneak into them rushes in front of the place. You should get some good pickings. Get a pale and walk through the big bog for cranberries. Carry your little single hammer shotgun in case a rabbit jumps up. We will go deer hunting for some proper nourishment when I get over there.

Dick Reed

I have not a doubt you are in need of supplies. Jay Clark says take the high land northeast til you run into the N.P. track. Follow your nose and watch the sun cant help but hit the track no fear of getting lost.

Rite the grocery order on a card and the r.r. section hands will take it to Cromwell and set the goods off by the track next day. Dont leave stuff sitting there too long for fear of light fingered folks. Might be the hands will let you go along in that case do so and you will not have to walk back next day. Dont try to tote more than eighty or ninety pounds on your wheelbarrow what with all them hills and woods you got to cut through.

Get 50 pound of salt pork 5 of sugar 5 of salt 2 of coffee and tea each and a few boxes of dried fruit and vegetables. Dont get the vegetables if money is short. Ask Pa if he may want a little tobacco for his pipe.

My hand is practical crippled from holding a scythe all day and writing this letter.

Fred Nielsen

P.S. Thought I heard a links holler early this morning. Night sounds are enough to make your hare stand on end.

Mpls
October 10, -92

Bror,

Got word of Fred the cabin was four logs high when it rained for a week and drowned you out. Said it was mighty cramped with the three of you back in that Merwin shack. He hopes he has spent his last night there. It's right thinking to move the house to higher ground. We're obliged to Mr. Clark and that Indian man what's his name for helping out as no telling when you'd get the place built by yourselves.

Say Marcus, the best way to get the deer is a fire hunt. Make a jack-o-lantern box with a sliding door. Fit it up inside with a thick tallow candle. At night row the boat quietly along the rushes with the open door pointed to shore. The deer's eyes shine in the dark and can be easy shot. Takes 2 to manage it so get Fred to go along.

Ma is awful lonely and her system is out of order.

Ole

P.S. Happy to hear Mr. Clark will help with your letters. Don't let Pa talk Norwegian to you.

Mpls
Nov 1, 1892

My Dear Marcus,

We felt awful to hear that Fred built the fire too high and the roof caught fire and your lien-to burnt up. You boys must have busted a mirror to be having such poor luck. We are praying the cabin will be ready when the real cold weather comes. Everything white here, snowflakes coming down outside the window are big as dollars.

Uncle Hans Friestad was telling about his visit to the "shack" when your helper, that big old grey lumberjack Tom Hull, decided he would get supper. You was off to Cromwell again, I guess. Anyway, he took the pail and made mush but it was dark by the time they got ready to eat. Mr. Hull used Birch Bark for dishes and spoons, have you still not found your stuff, and when it got warm the bark turned soft. When the fire was stoked, they saw Pa's whiskers were black from the mush! Guess it was some site.

I have got fleshy these past weeks but usually thin out in the cold months. The measles are all around thick. It will be queer if we don't get it.

Mrs. Ole Nielsen

Mpls
Dec. 8, 1892

Marcus,

Pa wrote it must've been seventy or eighty below the other night. Ole says to tell him if it got that cold he ought to be careful when he talks as his words will only freeze and fall to the ground. ha. ha.

I am sending woolen union suits, shirts, and mittens. Pa is to get the wool cap with earlaps like you boys.

Well, we are disappointed Pa decided you, he, and Fred will winter there alone. Ma took it hard but knows she is not fit to camp out in that cold. As Pa says, we must wait to come in the spring. Just so money don't give out.

Pa must have drew the picture of our new home in the dark. Ma asked to make sure of it.

held down by split saplings nailed along the edges. Is this what you call a scooped roof?

We see one four pane window each on the north and east walls, with the door on the south side. 3 downstairs rooms, a kitchen that can serve as a sitting or dining room, and 2 bedrooms, with wide puncheon floors throughout. Is the sleeping area in the loft to be reached by an outside stairway?

Now Marcus, take care the little house is raised up away from the spring, and that it is not poorly made, nor drafty. Can you get moss out of the woods to finish the chinking or is it froze?

Mrs. Ole Nielsen

P.S. Fred says you are skinny as a rail and have grown 1/2 a foot since summer. Eat more fat if you can get hold of it.

Five Friestad boys, unidentified, Fred on horse, Ole, original Nielsen house.

Pa's drawing looks to show the house is made of balsam and is eight logs high, with a loft and gabled roof, measuring fourteen by twenty-four feet. The scooped roof is covered with tar paper

Mpls
December 15, 1892

Marcus,

Your sister Josephine has determined you boys are to have a Lutefisk Holiday dinner and expressed up a bushel of potatoes, peas, flour, butter, sugar, and a big can of cod she already soaked and cured for a week. This is the way I make it for four -

Boil up the potatoes and peas and have lots of butter and bread ready and warming before you start. Cut up two pounds of the lye fish into good-sized chunks. Put four cups of water into a big skillet and bring it to a boil, drop in the fish, and simmer for a minute. Add two ounces of salt and simmer another five minutes, then ladle it on a plate. Make sure you add the salt after the fish has boiled. Should be just right if you paid attention.

Why don't you make some Lefse for dessert, use up the potatoes in some form besides boiled.

4

Better lay in some extra sugar if you can get hold of any.

We pray for you this holiday season. God Jul & Godt Nyttar!

Mrs. Ole Nielsen

Mpls
March 25th, 1893

Brother Marcus,

We finally got a letter from Pa where he said the snow has been so thick you've been holed up in the house for weeks and could do nothing but play pea nuckle. Said you were down to rabbit and pike through the ice for eats until the weather broke last week.

We will hold Ma here till end of April to let winter play out before coming up for good. Been hard on her but said all she needed was a long draught from the Fountain of Youth and would be fine. Well, you did say the spring has fine tasting water.

Ole

Mpls
April 6, '93

Marcus,

Ole says to figure on coffee, tea, sugar, salt, flour, and salt pork for store bought. All the rest we got to grow, catch, or shoot. Inquire of Mr. Clark as to whether there is a milch cow to be had for the babies.

Now as to digging the garden, you boys want to get a nice big piece of mellow ground worked up as soon as it thaws out. And tell Fred to start on the root cellar. Be sure of the soil so it will stay dry and cool. Make shallow bins bedded in sand to hold the carrots, turnips, and beets. Corn, beans, and peas will be dried before storing. Make bigger bins for the potatoes, rutabagas, onions, and parsnips. Pumpkins and squash can be set anywhere. Leave a place to build shelves for canned goods. Has anyone nearby an apple orchard?

I'm thinking of the deer, coons, and other critters apt to get into the garden. Put your thinking cap on and figure how to keep them out.

Hunt up as many open spots that can get plenty of sun, where we can put in extra potatoes. Mr. Gunderson told Fred potatoes can be shipped to St. Paul for cash.

The children took up with the grippe and are not fit to be around.

Mrs. Ole Nielsen

Mpls
May 4, 1893

Marcus,

Am sending new petticoats to replace the ones Ma ruined crossing the bog. She said her dress would clean up but her new shoes were soft as rags and that Pa threw them into the brush. And could you not have found a stiffer hat to hold the mosquito netting away from her face? She got all bit up. You ought to use more care where you run her.

Josie got word that sister Christine had been exposed to Small Pox but it was the 9th day when she wrote.

Ole is sending kerosene and 2 lamps by express so you may have something for light beside deer tallow candles. The cost is fearful so don't use it but when you can't get the other.

Tell Fred yes we would like him to come down and help move us up.

Mrs. Ole Nielsen

P.S. Your letter just arrived where Fred's pup, Lufra, drug Ma's shoes out of the woods but they could not be of any use. That swamp crossing was a fool thing.

Mpls
June 10, 1893

Marcus,

Oles and me are coming back in three days. Will come out by way of the high ground at the Sand Cut. Mr. Gunderson offered his yoke of ox he keeps in Sicottis old trading post.

5

Got more smudges, netting, etc. If you think the moskeetoes are bad near the house you ought to see what is in the swamp. Like to have carried me away. I think I am poisoned, feel poorly and have big sores all over. Why, them devils could drill through iron. Mr. Gunderson made up some turpentine and kerosene mixed with lard and spread it on the bites before I got on the train but didnt help much. No doubt you got a taste of same when you come to pick this up. Go home by way the Sand Cut. Keep the smudges going all the time around the house to stop them bog vultures from taking up by us.

    Fred

P.S. You know that Christly big white pine grove north of Tamarack? They cut one down 200 feet high at the crown over six feet thick at the trunk and loaded a section of it on a flatcar. Its waiting on the siding to be hauled to that big fair in Chicago. Take a look before you go home.

Virgin white pine nearly five feet thick.

Mpls
July 6, 1893

Brother Marcus,

    The tailor shop where Mr. Friestad works has nothing for him and we can't pay rent. Tell Pa and Ma and Ole's we are coming up on the 12th.

    We done all we could but it was of no use. Tell Pa what happened. You have a way of saying things where folks don't get their nose crooked. We aim to work for our keep no charity. It's just we can not afford a roof. $5 Bills do not grow on bushes these days, in fact they seem to hang higher than they ever did far as we're concerned.

    The boys are small but growing fast and can help out. The place will be crowded what with three families but can't be helped. I'm told Ole and his family have pitched a tent out in the yard and we will do the same.

    Søster Emma
    Mrs. H.J. Friestad

Jay Lake
Sept 1, 1893

Master Mark,

    Your Pa says he gave you a little time off "for good behavior." Clearing trees and grubbing stumps and rocks is real labor, certain. I expect your fingers are curled up solid and did someone have to pry loose the ax handle?

    Those white pine are some trees. When I came here in '81 they were so close together we had to chop some down to see the sun. I have been told the woods goes on to the north clear to Hudson's Bay.

    The Northern Pacific had some time as well when they cut through in '70. Story is two men and an engine sank in the swamp a mile east of Bill Sicottis' trading post and were never recovered. I don't know but what some of our bogs are bottomless.

Stop over and we will get in a little "learnin'." Your Pa said you had no formal schooling after the fifth grade so will take up from there.

Your friend,

Mr. Jay B. Clark

P.S. See if Mother Nielsen hasn't some bread to spare. You can take her back a few combs of honey. I have 27 swarms now.

Nielsen Lake
June 13, -94

Marcus,

Jay Clark has taken to calling our body of water Nielsen Lake as he says nobody by the name of Bass lives in these parts. Pa got a twinkle in his eye.

Mr. Friestad is building a little cabin on our new 40 acre homestead alongside your folks. The house has got too small. He wonders if Mr. Gunderson could spare you from wood chopping for awhile and can you come out to help him.

Emma

Mpls
Sept. 14th, 1894

Marcus,

Glad to hear the cold compresses worked and Pa's eyes cleared up and that you are making a fast recovery from the disaster. What of Ole's plans to get his own homestead? Last I heard he was thinking of filing to the west near a place called Sheriff Lake. Did that country burn up too?

Ma has asked that I come up for putting by, what with all the new work of rebuilding the barn, etc. on top of the regular fall smoking, canning & pickling, & such. It was awful lucky she had

harvested most of the garden and the root cellar wasn't damaged. I still marvel the house didn't burn down. They say hundreds got killed, mostly at Hinckley.

Josie

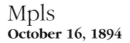

Mpls
October 16, 1894

Marcus,

Was very tired and hungry when I got home late last night. The engine broke down at Carlton and they could not get it fixed, on account I think the boiler fix it man was drunk. I slept until noon and it is 4 o'clock now and still feel like I have one foot in the grave and the other on a banana peel.

It was good to be with my family and am homesick now that I am back here. I think if I feel better I will go over to Christine's tomorrow. She always cheers me up.

Josie

P.S. There was a nice letter from Mr. Martin Tingdale. He has asked to pay a call.

Mpls
December 25th, 1894

Bro. Marcus and all,

Merry Christmas! And what a nice present for Emma - a healthy baby girl! Helga is a pretty name. Can it be so, as Mr. Clark said, that she is the first white baby born in your part of the country? What a fright that medical people up there are scarcer than Latin Scholars and Ma had to stand for nurse, doctor, and midwife!

I cannot help but remember those wonderful days visiting this summer and fall. If I close my eyes, I can see your lovely log home nestled along the shore, a northwest breeze driving the bugs down into the grass, and puffy white clouds crossing the blue sky. I can see Ole's and Friestad's camped in the yard, and all of us sat down to dinner in the house. I count seventeen men, women, and children squeezed in around the table!

I never slept as good as I did in your fresh open air, so different from the city. And I miss the early mornings when your pair of loons cut loose with their crazy woman call and woke us all up. I expect now they are sunning themselves on a beach at their winter home in the tropics.

It's grand that awful Hinckley fire spared the trees on the north side of your lake. When the water was still, the reflection of those great white pine on the water was almost as clear as the real things themselves.

I can see us hauling in pike by the tubful and going berry picking every morning before the sun got too high. There is so much plenty to be taken from Nature's Pantry. Remember the lazy afternoons when we laid in the sweet-smelling tall grass and listened to the red-wing blackbirds sing their songs? Then a quick swim in the lake before supper - oh my, but the water was cold!

I miss all that blue and green and the dazzling red maple and yellow oak leaves when all here is gray and white, and four or five more months of it to boot though of course it is winter there too and, silly me, I am only looking at things through rosecolored glasses.

Josie

Tamarack Section House
April 15, —95

Mark, if you want to make some extra money Devlin and John Anderson up to Round Lake are packing down a lot of fish to be shipped to St. Paul. What they want is the Pike, not the slimy pickerels, and are giving 3 cents a pound for dressed fish delivered here. Also they will be wanting the ruffled grouse so bring in all you can shoot. While here you can chop me some more wood as I'm low. Matron will feed you and fix a bed for the night.

Old Tom Hull is down from Murphy's Camp and sponging off Matron's table. Yesterday, he fell down chasing a bear and shot up two of his fingers. He cut away the shreds with a pen knife

but had to have Matron saw off the bones even. He went back out after the bear this morning.

B. Gunderson

P.S. I want you to help me give the section house, depot, and platform a fresh coat of red paint. N.P. says to paint over the old name of Sicottis and put Tamarack up there.

Sandy River Crossing
Sep. 3rd, 1895

Bro. Marcus,

Dick Reed gave the all right for a number of us to take a few days away from the haying and go ricing. The Injuns comeing through say there is a good crop up to Sandy Lake this year.

Will take canoes down the river into the big

flowage and work it Injun style. One man poles the boat through the rice beds while the fellow in front bends the stalks over with one stick and knocks the heads off with tother. The ripe rice drops into the boat. I will bring home what I can better ask Jay Clark if he knows how to parch the stuff.

Reed has been so used to asking extra men to help out he got surprised this year when they all showed up. No body has any money.

Fred

Tamarack Section House
November 16, 1895

Mark, there is a big demand for venison in Duluth and I have got deer stacked across my platform like cordwood. Fred and you ought to harvest what you can as prices are up and cannot say how long they will stay that way and they pay in hard cash.

As winter closes in, we will be getting more and more men down from the lumber camps, coming for their mail and the substantial Sunday dinner Matron is determined to give them. This week she will have raspberries, fried fish, and sourdough biscuits, plus blueberry pie - all they can put away. Has Mother Nielsen any yeast for to make bread? I hope Mother can come, Matron is going to ask 10 cents a meal from now on and will give Mother some of it if she will come by and help.

We hope to see you and bring along everyone and we can fill our bellies and I will tell some R.R. tales.

Mr. Gunderson

P.S. The N.P. pay car came thru and distributed gladness to all hands. I will hold your coin in my safe.

Cromwell, Minn.
December 20, 1895

Marcus,

Have you heard? That section hand Johnson was working the spike maul while Ben held a chisel and the maul got away from him and killed Gunderson. Some of the section boys don't like the smell of it but why would Johnson want to hurt Ben? Since it happened they say he has been acting as if he was 2 sandwiches short of a picnic.

Am staying over a couple days for the hardware and salt pork to come in. What we got left is pretty close to the edge.

Ole

Sandy River Crossing
March 13, 1896

Bro. Marcus,

Jay, John Maxwell, and I got back from trapping up to Sandy Lake and are holed up here. Got mostly wolf, links, and weasel, some fox, quite a little mink, and several bear. Mr. Clark said years ago beever was the thing around Sandy and they paid top dollar for it but now not worth the taking even if you could find them. Will finish the pelts and ship to Aitkin as the train stops here now. Wont get as much as had hoped for two months out in the dam cold but will have to do.

Ran into Ole this morning. He had a time on a grocery trip to Moose Lake. A day over and more than a day back toteing a 100 pound sack of flour with more in his pack. A fingerboard at a fork was pointed the wrong way and he proceeded down a little used trail and got lost in the dark. Walked all night and drug himself into the house at dawn near froze to death.

Fred

P.S. Say, a section hand said after that fellow Johnson went crazy from the killing he come out of it over the winter and married Ben Gunderson's widow.

Jay Lake
April 15, 1896

Mark,

Enjoyed your stay this past week, as I always do. Hope your head isn't still "aching" from all the schooling. Keep working on the figures as you have a head for numbers that could stand you well if you go into business.

Now young fellow, I know you aren't happy with farming but your Pa needs you and I know you won't let him down by running off at every chance on a carnelian hunt. It is true he's little account as a farmer but even with Ole gone to his own claim on Sheriff Lake there is still Fred so it's not as if you had the whole load yourself.

Mr. Clark

P.S. John Maxwell owed it was a panther that came into his camp and stole the deer. Better keep an eye peeled.

Sheriff Lake
June 15th, 1896

Bro. Marcus,

I am about as far behind as the caboose with all the work around here. But we got two acres in potatoes, ten in oats, and the garden's planted full.

Well, I bought a chunk team of another settler. The both of them come out of an old alley cat mare but their sire was a percheron. I want to cut & haul wood for Murphy this winter. Sure hope it works out. Money is scarcer than dollar growing strawberry trees.

Some say we oughten to look over this Mr. William Jennings Bryan from Nebraska. Expect he couldn't run the country no worse. Fellow across the lake says it stacks up to "Gold-Bug" McKinley vs "Free Silver" Bryan. I don't hardly know what he's talking about.

Ole

Jay Lake
July 19, 1896

Mark,

You asked about hunters and trappers of olden times and how it was we got the news and happenings of the day. Well, twas nothing to it, my boy.

Each man along the lakes and rivers had him a particular rock set in shallow water. Along side of that rock was set a sounding board made of a certain wood tilted just so. What a fellow did was take another particular kind of rock and whang at the rock in the water. The sound came out of the water and bounced off the board into the ether. It would travel for miles, with each man along the way relaying the message until it got to it's final destination. Worked as good as any telegraph of today, maybe better.

J.B. Clark

Tamarack
August 27, 1896

Brother Marcus,

Was up to Round and Horseshoe Lakes looking things over til haying starts at Reeds. There are quite a number of homesteaders up that way now - Barotts, Devlins, Fishers, and Simeon and John Anderson. A prairie schooner went by last night with another load. The country is filling up.

Fred

Jay Lake
Sept. 11th, '96

Mark,

I am down from a hunting and fishing trip to Sandy Lake. Twas a poor hunt but netted a good deal of fish which I smoked up to the Indian Village. I gave them half and still have too much. Better come over and help eat some up.

I see they finally finished that fool gov't dam over at the outlet river to the Mississippi. The lake is a good three or four feet higher than it was before they closed the doors. Swallowed up plenty of sand beach I can tell you. The Indians don't care for it and neither do I - it will change the lake, hurt the fishing and ricing, and generally muss things up. Gov't claims it's got to control the big river for everybody down stream and I guess that says it all. They already have other dams at Pine, Pokegama, Leech, and Big Winnie so I expect Minneapolis now owns all our water.

J.B. Clark

Mississippi River near Sandy Lake.

In the 1820s, Henry Schoolcraft wrote the Ojibway built their campfires on this point on Sandy Lake, directly opposite the Prairie River.

Carlton, Minn.
March 16, 1897

Marcus & folks,

    Got here late morning and am camped out in the N.P. depot as I cannot afford a hotel room. Expect to return day after tomorrow with harnesses, etc., at least four crates of chickens, groceries, and lumber for my new milkhouse.

    Marcus, my barn roof has sagged from all the weight brought on by this "Winter Of Much Snow." Leave off your r.r. section work for a few days and help me straighten it before she caves in.

    Ole

Mpls
May 18, '97

Bror Marcus,

    It is your 18th birthday and I expect you consider yourself a man for you certainly are acting like one of the specie. It was one thing to quit the farm, but quite another to change your name to Nelson. Pa says Fred has done the same and he does not know why you are ashamed of the name Nielsen.

    What are you to do in Tamarack? Pa says you have gone back to the Merwin shack. That filthy old place is so small you could faint and not fall down. I don't know how you stand it.

    Pa thought you might "cruise" for a logging outfit. Do you know how to do that?

    Pa and Ma want to hold on to the homestead, but not sure how it will work what with you and Fred run off. Pa proves up this fall and wants to get his Homestead Patent.

    Josie

P.S. Oh yes, Mr. Martin Tingdale has asked to marry me.

N.P. section crew.

Sheriff Lake
June 23, 1897

Bro. Marcus,

Have planted my corn three times on account of hail. Next year will stick to oats and rye as it is a joke to try and grow corn, or even wheat. A fellow come through and said that down in Ioway all they got to do is scratch the land with a hoe to get 50 bushel an acre. Said they'd plant silver dollars but for fear of getting a crop of eagles. Said it with a straight face he did.

All wore out grubbing stumps and picking rock. Frank Carlson told me a glacier from ancient times dumped its load of stones off here & I don't doubt it. I am beginning to think one crosses over the place nightly. I used to believe what they say about trees following the fertile ground but I'm cured of that.

We had hoped the longer summer days would make up for the short growing season. The soil is awful sour, and I ought to lime it but have not the money. So little black dirt and so much rock, clay, and sand, no wonder the yields are pitiful. Where we can get something to grow, it stays wet all season and can't get it out. The countryside ought to be ditched so lower ground is fit to farm.

Ole

P.S. Somebody said they saw John Anderson skinning the logs north of Tamarack with a plow on his back.

Sandy River Crossing
August 28, 1897

Marcus,

Yesterday some dandy got off the N.P. and asked of our "road system." Wanted to rent a rig and "have a leesurely excurzion up to Sandy Lake." Tom Reed laughed so hard he hurt.

One of the boys finally told him alls there was up there was game and redskin trails and heed have to travel by way of shanks mare. The fellow

got bug eyed at the mention of Injuns and jumped back on that train just as it was pulling away. Twas more fun than Ive had since the cowcatcher had a calf.

Dont know how many more years Reed can make hay here. The Grass Twine Company is buying up all the savannas for use to making twine and mats and the like. Well that wire grass makes better rope than feed to be sure.

Fred

Sheriff Lake

Aug 29 of 97

Mr. Marcus Nelson,

My family thank you for help when train land in Tamarack. It is terrible to come to wilderness in middle of night from so far away. We grateful you take us in your little house no matter there no place for any to sleep but floor. Poor night sleep small price for roof and good talk about our new life.

Thank for sharing breakfast. Children thought it funny we could eat but two at a time without washing plate or mug. Thank for guide to our place. Reason seven year old Amanda who cannot understand English good was so scared when you backtracked to find right trail was she thought you had left us there to die. If you had not made us stay still until you found path we would surely been lost in that deep woods.

My husband has put up leen-to while we build our house. Have many fine neighbors most have helped one way or other. Your brother Ole and wife very kind.

Enclosed $1 find money so little for so much. Next time you come south I cook a dinner.

I am, gratefully,
Mrs. Oscar Sundberg

McGregor, Minn.

October 15, 1897

Mr. Marcus Nelson, Esq.
Tamarack, Minn.
Sir:

Jay Clark says you are a good man with an axe and reliable. If you are looking for woods work this winter be at my Drive Camp one mile north of the Prairie River mouth on Nov. 23rd and give this letter to my clerk. We will go in soon as the river freezes over. Tell your people you won't be out till May, as I will need you to come down river with the wood.

Jim Murphy

Friestad's

Nov 19, 1897

Brother Marcus,

After all these years of living with your folks, then that dark hole of a little shack next to them, we have finally moved into a new frame house. I thought it would never happen but now that it is here what a glorious day! There are three rooms downstairs and a good stairway to the second floor. The upstairs isn't finished but we plan two good-sized bedrooms. Mr. Clark told H.J. we had built our roof so tall & steep J.B. feared the flies would hold sliding bees every Sunday afternoon. Ha! Ha!

We have moved in our stove, beds, a table, trunk, and two chairs. You remember that long-handled fry pan Fred gave me when we lived at

Hans Julius Friestad wearing tie, Emma sitting, and several children.

the old shack, the one I had either to keep the door open or no one could sit on the chair between the stove and table? Well, there's no call to have to move around it now. I have the finest, roomiest kitchen in this part of the country!

When you come out next, I will make fried chicken your favorite with all the trimmings.

Joyfully, Emma

Nielsen Lake
June 15, 1898

Dear son Marcus in tamarack

    yesterday after 18 years of living in this country i become citizen. i put day off for long becoss i could no belief i would live in US for rest of life. this i come to no at last and so have done it.

hard part was oath wen i must "renounce Norway." Whi use such word? i love country of birth and feel traytor. but would be harder without citizen for i could not feel like reel American. i hope my new broom sweeps clean - nye koster feier best.

    we go home right after as i feel not well.
    yours truly Fader

P.S. i pray God i have done rite ting bringing you children to America.

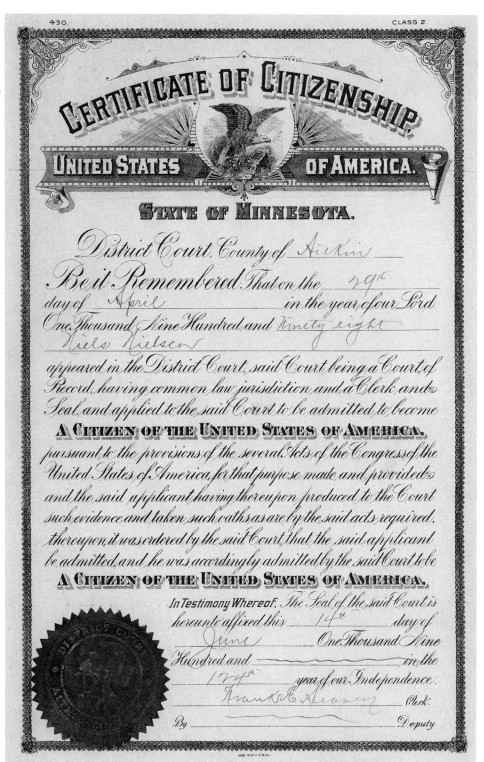

Note the Certificate's date error.

McGregor
Nov 14th, 1898

Bro. Marcus,

    Finally got the dope on that "Indian Massacre." You recollect we heard they had attacked & wiped out McGregor. Well what happened a Indian butchered a deer and stopped at a farm to clean up. The woman of the place - her man was off - jumped to the conclusion the savage had just finished chopping somebody up and was about to start on her. She tore off in a rig screaming like a banshee and stirred up the whole countryside. Half the settlers skedaddled. One old bird who sat the whole thing out wittlin in a chair told me the pore old town injuns were peeking out doors with their jaws hanging down. A few hours later everybody come mopeing back with their tales between their legs. Theres plenty of red faces around here but they dont belong to no Injuns!

    Fred

McGregor
April 19, '99

Bro. Marcus,

Did odd jobs this winter for food and roof but cannot make any money. May have been I should have gone up with Murphy too but could not bring myself to it. I like crewsing and hauling but not the axe and saw work.

Some of Reed's injuns stopped by and asked if I wanted to go gather sugar water from the maples. They drive wood spouts into the trees and let the sap drip into pans then boil it up in big kettles leaving nothing but syrup. If get any will bring some to you and the folks.

Fred

Sheriff Lake
May 17th, 1899

Marcus,

Somebody said you and Tingdale have started to build a store in Tamarack. Maybe you can bring some extra grub out to Friestad's now that Ma and Pa are staying with Emma. The two of them are in bad shape. Pa told Fred he is fed up at being burned out twice and is going to move back to Mpls.

Had another bad spell here too. Lost both our sows to some foul disease and the piglets followed. Went just like that without their maw's. Then the cow's milk went bad after she got into something in the woods. The Mrs. has bust out with hives over it all.

The soil on my place is about played out. If we don't get a decent crop this year I may be in about the same fix as Ma and Pa.

Ole

Sheriff Lake
July 5, 1899

Brother Marcus,

Yesterday was a ray of sunshine in what has been a sorry year. Dick Reed had us up to a big Fourth of July celebration at his place at Sandy River Crossing. Some eight or ten families were there.

Barott's come in dug out canoes by the water route all the way from Round Lake. They had a lively trip. Hiked over to Horseshoe Lake, thru the channel into Rice Lake, then down Rice Creek into Sandy River. Must be some 12 or 14 miles by water. Said the eatbodies were just terrible till they got a smudge to working. We learned later pulling against the Sandy River current took the fiddling ambition out of Pat Barott to a certain percent.

There was a picnic at 1:00 PM. Jimmy Green, Murphy's camp cook that everybody likes so well, baked up a storm - bread, donuts, cakes, and pies. We ate till we nearly busted. They had games for children in the afternoon followed by stunts of physical skill. Gust Amundson come out the best when he made himself into a stiff board, feet on one chair & head on another. Frank Clark stood on him but could not make him bend.

Reed and some of the boys built a bowery for dancing, with a nice platform and roof. We all gathered near it at dusk and lit off whatever cartridges and powder we felt could be spared. We finally got "Pat the Fiddler" to work and everybody shook a leg - waltzing, two step, square dance, shottish, polka dance, coming thro the rye, and the menu et. We danced till midnight when by general agreement it was time to go home.

Ole

Friestad's
Aug 13, 1899

Marcus,

You ought to know a fearful Hailstorm hit us about 12 o'clock yesterday. Hailstones as big as walnuts come down with heavy rain after it. I was holding Baby Girl looking out the window when I noticed tar paper flying into the woods. Didn't take long before the covering of my house lay in the brush on the nearby 40.

Haakon and Anker had gone to the folks' place to tend the garden, but Fred seen the weather and told them to hurry home. What a sight they were! Anker was crying and both were beaten up by the hail. There were red spots all over their bodies. I bawled awhile myself when the water come tumbling down my bedroom steps.

Better leave off your town work and take a hike out here. Pa and Ma are awful low.

Emma

McGregor
Nov. 25, 1899

Marcus,

That team I bought to haul wood give completely out on me. The both of them laid down in the snow and wouldnt get up. I knew they werent too likely but the man I bought them of said they could take on short hauls.

One of Murphys tote teams come by picked me up shot the horses and collected the harness & rigging I borrowed of Murphy. I am now broke and without a clue. When a fellow gets to offering you something that sounds too good to be true then its time to get on home and lock the smokehouse. But I am a hard headed Norske and will probably never learn.

Am headed for Oles. Will cut through the swamp as I expect Jack Frost has come along and petrified it. The deer are ripe and ready for picking so will try and harvest one so as not to come in empty handed.

Fred

Mpls
June 22, 1900

Bro. Marcus,

I have not had a chance to write since giving up the Sheriff Lake farm as a bad job. We have pulled out and the place is up for sale. Toward the end I felt like the company man who started at the bottom and worked his way down. As the fellow said, it was a case of the farm owning the farmer.

We are staying with Pa and Ma down here and I am looking for work. They have got a nice frame house and Pa has got hold of some carpentry work. Say, see what can be done about renting his farm as he can not bear to part with it.

Josie said got word of Fred and that he has gone off to Duluth on another of his bright ideas.

Ole

PART TWO

Sixteen-year-old Mamie Barnett is at the upper right corner. Others are her sisters, brothers, and cousins. Nineveh, Indiana, March 18, 1896.

Nearly eight hundred miles to the southeast, the Benjamin F. and Mary Ellen Barnett family were living on a large farm near Franklin, Indiana. They had eleven children: Ida, Cora, Dilla, Maggie, Deocia, Humboldt, Myrtle, Daisy, Mamie, Kate, and Frank. While the others were content to lead conventional lives, twenty-year-old Mamie Sophronia Barnett was full of wanderlust. In the spring of 1899, much to her family's horror, the fiesty little Hoosier packed her bags and headed west - alone! In the fall of 1900, she traveled to Tamarack at the request of her sister Deocia, whose husband, Ed Lilliedale, was then local N.P. Section Foreman.

Due to the acute shortage of single women, it wasn't long before Mamie attracted the attentions of Marcus Nelson. At the same time Fred Nelson became acquainted with Simeon Anderson's daughter, Annie. Nature took its course and the two couples married in 1901. After daughter Myrtle and son Orvis were born, Mamie and Marcus adopted Gust Oja, an orphaned Finnish boy. Jay Clark and a beloved hired man, Dennis Carr, became members of the immediate family. "Uncle Marcus" and "Aunt Mamie", as the other settlers referred to them, assumed leadership of the growing community.

Tamarack was becoming a regular settlement, with an increasing demand for good roads and schools. Missionaries brought the Gospel and established churches. Marcus and his brother-in-law, Martin Tingdale, opened Tamarack's first store in 1899. Ed Douglas, a logger from Aitkin, opened a second general mercantile within a year or two. In 1902 Marcus bought Tingdale out, expanded the store, and got into the timber business himself. Still in his twenties, the man baptized as Niels Marcus Nielsen prospered beyond his dreams.

Mamie at age eighteen.

Marcus & Mamie in their Tamarack lumber yard.

Left to right: N.P. section house, depot, Merwin shack, Sicottis' old trading post,
Tingdale/Nelson store. Sicottis' old well is at lower right corner.

The "old" store

Strutting the boardwalk. Children were still rare at Tamarack.

Marcus is scooping bulk goods into a sack on the scale.

1899 to 1904

*Marcus holds his dog Topsy, surrounded by a collection of his customers.
Notice the outdoor thermometer above man to Marcus' left. The man in
foreground appears to have whittled his stick to the bone.*

*(L to R) Charley Anderson and his father, Simeon Anderson, Martin Tingdale, Frank Barnett,
Marcus. Simeon was killed in the woods shortly after this picture was taken.*

Tamarack N.P. Section House
Sept 1, 1900

Mr. Nelson,

You may have heard Miss Annie Anderson has left our employ to go back to her folk's place on Anderson Lake and my wife's sister, Miss Mamie Barnett, has arrived to look after things while Deocia is in a family way. Miss Barnett is a sturdy young Hoosier woman, your age, who went west looking for adventure and spent last winter teaching on the Nebraska prairie where she lived in a sod house. She had hoped to get a better position but could not with but an eighth grade education and so now she has come to us.

Miss Barnett has indicated a desire to sight see the area and I can think of no better guide. Why don't you stop by for supper tomorrow and talk it over.

    Ed Lilliedale
    Section Foreman

Miss Forsythe, on left, and Annie Anderson at the section house.

The Lilliedales. Little Juanita (foreground) was named after a popular tune of the day.

25

Tamarack Section House
Sept 10, 1900

Mr. Marcus Nelson, Esq.
Dear Sir:

Am obliged for steering me around Tamarack. I wonder if I might impose once again. Have heard a good deal about Chippewa Indians at Sandy Lake and would like to see some. On account of your horse and road shortage I am told a body must walk up that way some twelve miles over rough ground so Mr. Lilliedale said. I am toughened up from my stay out West so no need to concern yourself I could not stand the trip.

Would you be off-handed if I wore a breeches outfit? Skirts and petticoats are no match for your woods and I have a pair I made myself.

Kindly inform Mr. Lilliedale of your disposition and with respects, I am,
Yours truly,
Miss Mamie Barnett

Zion's Hill
Horseshoe Lake
Sept 17, 1900

Mr. Nelson, Manager
Tingdale Store, Tamarack

Well, we are here and mighty glad to put our grips away. Mrs. James Barott has given our rise of ground a name, Zion's Hill, on account she fancies it overlooks her own Promised Land.

Skinning the logs across the swamp north of Tamarack was a trial for all but more so for the children Elise and Percy. Elise was carrying a

yellow canary and could not keep her balance & hold the cage at the same time. James Barott, who was waiting for us with his wagon on the high ground, laughed when he saw Elise all covered with mud and the girl broke into tears. But little Ethel Barott made up for it when she squealed with delight at her little bird present.

The tote road up here is about the roughest I've seen. Powerful generous to call it a road atall. We bounced so hard over ruts & stumps that everybody finally got out & walked while Barott led the team. By the time we got to Round Lake we were dried out and stopped at Devlin's well. That is the sweetest water I ever drank!

We have a fine spot tucked into a tall pine grove, mixed with paper birch. From one window we can see Horseshoe Lake. I have lined up steady work in Superior and will take up there next week, coming home on weekends.

Joseph Cayo

Tamarack Section House
October 5th, 1900

Marcus,

Won't you come to the Section House Sunday next? Mrs. Lilliedale is putting on a taffy pull and Miss Barnett is to conduct parlor games. We would expect a dozen souls from around the country if all can make it.

Ed Lilliedale

P.S. If the store has a little extra molasses bring it along.

Mpls
Feb 5, 1901

Bro. Marcus,

Have not heard from you since Xmas. We got that picture Miss Barnett made of you sitting outside with her sisters. Fred wrote that you have been spending a great deal of time over to the section house.

Josie

Franklin, Indiana
March 20, 1901

Mr. Marcus Nelson, Esq.
Tamarack, Minn.
Sir:

I have herewith in hand your letter of the 17th instant. requesting permission to marry my daughter Mamie. Mamie is my third youngest child and though not yet twenty-two has the head of a body considerably older. She can be independent on occasion, as you may have already woke up to. But she is the apple of my eye and I trust you will keep that in mind in your dealings with her.

I have only Mr. Lilliedale's say so on your character, but he gives me no call to question it and I must be satisfied with that.

You say you aim to get married this May in Duluth. I am sorry to say that none of us here have the time or money and cannot come.

Mama and I are wishing you children our best.

Benjamin F. and Mary E. Barnett

McGregor, Minn.
Apr. 15th, '01

Bro. Marcus,

Ran into Mr. E. L. Douglas of Aitkin who is getting active in the timber business at our end of the county. He wants me to cruise that fine run of pine along the Sandy River headwaters south of Tamarack. Mr. Douglas owed he would pay oxen skidders $15 a month he provide the ox. I signed on for next fall.

I stumbled onto Simeon Andersons lake up to T49-R23 last December. His daughter Annie has filled out considerable since last I saw her at the section house. Well, eats are hard to come by in the winter woods and they were kind enough to feed me whenever I come by which got kind of regular like after the New Year.

Do you know of any steady summer work?
Fred

Tingdale Bros. Realty
Mpls
May 12, 1901

Marcus,

Josie received Mamie's letter as to your marriage at the Methodist Church in Duluth and congratulations are in order. I understand that no other family members could be there and that only Mamie's friend, Miss Forsythe, was able to witness the event. Well, you know we were thinking of you.

Mamie said the boys in town organized a shivaree when you came back on the night train but that while they were hooting and hollering you slipped out the other side of the car and sneaked into the section house. Hope they weren't too upset they lost out on their fun.

I just read her letter again and it's clear your new wife is no shrinking violet. Yes, I will hire her to help at the store as it has become too much for one. But she asks too much at $15 a month. I can afford to pay $10. Is there room for the both of you to live in the back room?
Martin Tingdale

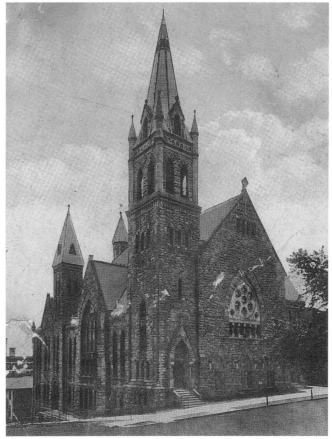

Waukegan, Ill.
June 15, 1901

Mr. Nelson:

The book "True Manhood, A Manual of Sexual Science," by E. R. Shepherd is an indispensable guide for young men to health, strength, and purity. No longer will you be "in the dark" about matters pertaining to your own body. And, as you can see from our leaflet, the book is endorsed by many prominent social leaders and clergymen. The price is one dollar prepaid.

On account of the peculiar class of this book many of our patrons have suggested we arrange a private address in writing us, which we enclose. This will enable you to communicate with us with no possibility of anyone knowing the nature of the business, or with whom you are dealing. And, naturally, the item will be shipped in a plain wrapper.

Hygiene & Tokology Co.

Friestad's
July 20, 1901

Brother,

I hear Mamie aims to commense a Sunday School in the back of the store. It is high time. We have all gone too long in this wilderness without the Word of God. H.J. and I will do all we can to get folks to send over their young ones and maybe stay and learn a few things themselves.

Emma

Franklin
December 25, 1901

Husband,

I am lonely on this Holy Day because you are far away. I miss you a great deal and will not stay longer than second week of January. All here tolerably well. Sister Myrtle had the grip but coming out of it.

Now Marcus do not spend so much time in the woods with your cruising work so as to neglect other things. If your lungs get to bothering you then by all means get out of the store. But ask a man to look after things till you get back.

Keep after the barrel stove as I believe the chimney is stopped up. It don't quite line up and the fire quits for want of draft. Do not let it freeze in there, will spoil the goods.

Mama is having another spell and must go. I will write a better letter tomorrow, she has made me cranky.

Love,
Your Wife
P.S. I drew a picture of what I consider a better kind of stove.

Franklin
January 10, 1902

Husband,

Coming home on the 14th inst. am happy to say. Mama is taking my leaving as well as can be expected.

Sister Myrtle and I went shopping to Indianapolis a few days ago. I bought a nice blue dress and two white shirt waists for everyday. We stopped in Franklin on way out to home and I bought another camera from man who taught me. Gave him my old one as part trade. Got more developing chemicals, print paper, glass plates, and a new black cloth to replace the one Topsy chewed up. Hope have not spent too much but all seem to enjoy my pictures and could not get the old camera to work to suit me.

Your Wife

Duluth Presbytery
Synod of Minnesota
October 29, '02

Mr. Marcus Nelson,

The Brother Jameson and I have accepted the Call to provide spiritual guidance to the settlers and lumber men in your community. We "sky pilots," as the camp men call us, will be conducting church services once a month. Your name was provided to us as someone we might ask to arrange meeting places. Usually this is done on a rotating basis from home to home, or in schools or halls if they are available. We should not think this too onerous a task and look forward to hearing from you.

Your most humble servant,
Brother Samuel Blair
Presbyterian Missionary

Franklin
July 24th, 1902

Sister Mamie,

Ma is getting to feel tolerably well again. She has been in and out of the sick bed for days. She said one night last week she laid down on her bed and tried to die but could not.

Cousin Chester Barnett confessed Christ and was baptized a few weeks ago. I was so glad to see him take that step, and hope it will help him get his life in order. I long for the time when our brothers will accept Christ as their guide and let Him pilot their bark safely to the other shore.

Protracted meeting began at the M.E. Church at Nineveh Tues. night. Already 5 or 6 have accepted Our Lord and Saviour Jesus Christ and still have two weeks to go. They have a nice neat building now.

Your sister, Myrtle Barnett
P.S. Pa got the letter saying Markus had bought out Mr. Tingdale's Tamarack interests.

Franklin
December 4, 1902

Markus,

I was delighted to get a letter from you. It was good of you to tell us about your life with Mamie. It must be exciting to be such a big part of building a new town.

Yes, Frank and I live at the home farm with Pa and Ma as we are the only ones not yet married. Tell Mamie I am sorry to see Nellie go too. Yes, she was broke well and gentle but Frank never liked the shape of her head and thought her ears too large. His new horse is a sorrel and very pretty.

We have had new R.F.D. routes established from out of Franklin and our No. is changed to No. 5 now. But we have the same carrier.

Let us hear more from you.
Your sister, Myrtle Barnett

Franklin
January 12, 1903

Markus and Mamie,

Sleet last night was rather hard on the winter wheat.

Frank has missed the measles but it is everywhere all around. He thinks he has had two or three chances. I wish we were over it.

We butchered this week. Pa & Daisy rendered the lard, Ma and Frank made sausage, and I looked on. Yesterday, Ma made a kettle of soap. She has 40 young chickens and 20 hens a setting.

I've been sick for over a week with a complication of La Grippe, pleurisy, and kidney trouble. I'm better but am so sore and weak, can't eat to do any good so I'm not any account yet.

Myrtle

P.S. Markus, I hope you are feeling stronger. Don't you think you should hunt up a doctor and have him listen to your lungs?

Franklin
February 23, 1903

Markus & Mamie,

I am more like my old self this past week. Frank & I received a beautiful valentine post marked Tamarack for which we are likely indebted to you ha ha.

Grandmother Sophronia Barnett is still here and sends her love. Whenever she speaks of you Mamie she always wonders if she'll live to get to see you again. Of course she's old born in 1817 just after the second war with England but is hardy and may live a good many years yet. None of us know when we'll go Home. The Darkie will drive her back to her place on Friday.

Myrtle

Zion's Hill
March 30, 1903

Marcus,

When you was out here cruising you had said you wanted to hear more about Grandpa's time during the big Indian war. I had the missus write it down -

"I, Alfred Barott, swear this is a true story of my times during the Indian troubles of 18 and 62. I had a farm in southern Minnesota and was considered friendly toward the Indians. Some time before it began, they told me that in so many moons they would begin to kill the palefaces.

"Well, I got the family together and we made for Fort Ridgely. While they poked along in the ox cart, I scouted ahead on my pony. I spotted a band of 14 Indians waiting to ambush us. Fortunately for me, they was poorly armed. I spurred the pony & rode them down, letting fly with my old Navy Colt. I hit 3 or 4 of them and threw the fear of God into the rest. After a couple of minutes, they disappeared over a rise. If my piece had been of heavier caliber, there'd a been some of them left on the ground.

"I got the family to the fort & the Indians attacked. They were getting the best of us until one quick-thinking boy rolled a barrel of whiskey out to them. While the Injuns stopped the battle to get drunk we sent a runner to Fort Snelling and managed to hold out till help arrived. Twas the only time I ever saw whiskey do any good."

Grandpa got wound up and told some stories I'd never heard. He remembered a time when he was hunting meat for the Libby and Rogers camp. Night overtook him and he settled down to sleep leaning against a tree. The timberwolves gathered around & he could not find enough firewood to drive them off, so he had to roost in a tree like a spruce hen. Said it hurt his feelings. "A bunch of wolves put me to roost & I like to froze to death."

Another time he had dug a lot of jinsing and stored it in his cabin. He was gone for a day and returned to find it missing. Sign told him somebody stole it. He hurried off and easy caught up with the man because he was heavy loaded down. Grandpa circled around to get in front of him and stuck his hat out on a stick from behind a tree. Bang! and a bullet went through the hat. I can do better than that, thought Grandpa. He lowered down on his sights and shot the thief between the eyes. He went to Duluth and reported to the Sheriff. They said it had been him or the other fellow and to go on back and bury him.

Your friend, Pat Barott

Tingdale Bros.
Mpls
Oct. 15th, 1903

Marcus,

Dumb Swede jokes have been making the rounds -

"Did you hear about the Dumb Swede who took his nose apart to see what made it run?"

"Know why the Dumb Swede took hay to bed with him? To feed his nightmare."

"What did the Dumb Swede do when told he was dying? Moved into the living room."

Martin

Franklin
March 31, 1904

My Dear Daughter,

I will send that money in a registered letter Mamie. You know that I would never be satisfied until I give all the married children the same. I have plenty of money now to gett all I kneed and more too. I sell my milk and creamery takes the butter out and brings me back the milk. It makes me five or six dollars in too weeks. I sell about fifteen dozen eggs in a week so it does not take long to gather up a sum of money.

You ask about rugs. It takes too pound of cotton raggs to a yard wide carpett and ten pound of ragg chains for twenty five ydz of carpett but I would advise you to sell your raggs and buy a carpett. I never will make a rag carpett if can gett it at cost. I think you had better not try to make one for you have so mutch to do.

Don't know if we can come to Tamarack. It puzels me what to do, for I will not go away and leave Myrtle. She can wash dishes and set the table and dust but I sweep and do all the hard work. You cannot get a girl to work for love or money. They are not to be had eny more. All work at something else, of course. I do not blame them.

A mother's love to you both.

Ma Barnett

P.S. That painter man finished the picture of our house. Little people look funny.

Franklin
April 14, 1904

Marcus,

Mamie arrived a few hours before the funeral and we were so thankful, for her strength helped us all get through an awful day.

We cannot a one of us believe our gentle & beautiful sister has left this world. She was such a loving, caring soul and always concerned for others and not herself. Myrtle Violet Barnett died on April 11, 1904, aged 29 years and 12 days.

She had been run down for so long that when she contracted measles her system could not deal with it. We are very mad at Frank for being so careless and allowing himself to be exposed.

Mamie says not to worry about her "condition" and that she will write in a day or two when fit.

Daisy

Franklin
May 14, 1904

Husband and Father,

Baby girl born yesterday 7 lbs, 5 oz. and appears healthy in every way. I cannot say she looks like either of us but is beautiful to me. Dear husband, I have decided on her name and will trust and believe you approve. She is to be Myrtle Barnett Nelson, after my late, beloved sister.

I would expect to be ready to travel in a week but will consult Dr. before hand so no need to write a high handed letter to the country at large regarding same. ha. Yes I would like for you to come get us and Pa says Marcus come any time.

Your loving wife, Mamie

P.S. Mama been feeling poorly, no appetite. She took Myrtle's passing awful hard. I been carrying around her last letter and reading it every day.

Mpls
May 18th, 1904

Mi Dear Son -

Woke in morning and found mi youngest child quarter century old. make me old but am thank full all mi children survive in new land. i see Oles as they do not live so far by city car. others good.

got letter of Mamie in Indiana. Mama so glad. small news only wish to you Happy Birthday. riting hand stop from stif.

Far and Mor

Duluth Presbytery
May 24, '04

Friend Marcus,

After services in Tamarack Sat. afternoon, I will walk out to the Barott school on Round Lake for an evening service. Can you ask Cayo's to put me up Sat. night? Sun. will be at Pine Ridge School, then an evening meeting in Haugen Township. Will spend Sun. night at Odegard's and return to Duluth Mon. morning. There are coming up to Balsam Town a number of new settlers I hope to somehow see before long.

Marcus, I thank you for your good offer to cart me around but I cannot have it. You are very busy and important to the welfare of your community and I could not abide myself if I allowed you to take off two valuable days so that I may be carried about as a Sultan. I am blessed with two sound legs and shall use them.

Brother S.A. Blair

P.S. Can you not draw me out mosquito netting for hat and bed. I can't seem to locate where I packed mine away last fall.

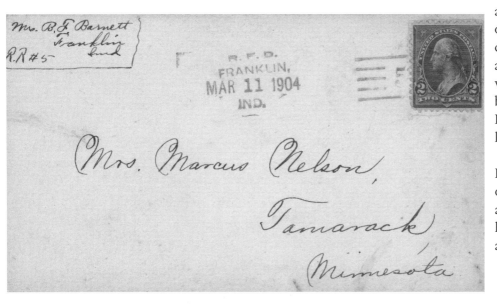

Myrtle always put her mother's name on the return address.

33

Eastern Aitkin County settlers.

Duluth Presbytery
May 30, '04

Marcus,

The service at the Pine Ridge School service was a most wonderful experience. All the fine people, beautiful sunny day, picnic tables laden with great quantities of fine food. I must confess I could almost become "intoxicated" by the scent of fresh cut lumber. It is everywhere in your country.

After we ate, Mrs. Jacobsen told of something that happened last Saturday forenoon. A well dressed young man carrying a little girl about four years of age stopped at the Jacobsen place on Round Lake and asked if he could buy a glass of milk for his little girl and a bite to eat for both of them. She was such a cute little girl in a pretty white dress and had the prettiest black hair. The father told the Jacobsen's that his little girl had been staying with relatives since her mother's death, but now he had made arrangements so he could have her with him and had gone after her. This father carried the little girl from Tamarack up to Sandy Lake for the sake of having her with him. They were Indians.

We sometimes think of them as savages without hope of redemption but I do not believe this is at all so. When time permits, I hope to bring the Word up to their village.

Brother Blair

P.S. Friend Marcus, what can I do to induce you to join Mamie & attend one of our services?

Tamarack
June 7, 1904

Brother Marcus,

Annie & I have decided to build a house in town. I want to take that spot about a hundred feet south of where you are building your new store so dont let nobody else in there.

Our little Alice is well. Baby Ernest has been troubled with colic ask Mamie if she cant mix up one of her famous nostrums and take it out. Better have her bring Myrtle as Alice has found out about her.

Fred

Franklin
Jan. 17, 1905

Children,

We buried Mama yesterday in the little plot she always wanted to rest in. She asked at the end we not worry you until it was all over as it was too much for you to try and come down here. She was only 62 years old but her life was not worth living any more and I believe she was glad to die.

Mary Ellen Middleton Barnett was born in this country but her folks came from north of Ireland where the Protestants live. They had been there for 99 years but their lease was out. Her Uncle Dion helped guard Napolian at Isle of Helena. Her parents died of spotted fever when she was little, and her cousin and elder brother stood for father and mother. Mama had a hard early life.

We married on August 18, 1864 at time of War of the Rebellion. We had 11 fine children, with 10 living, for which we were thankful to the Lord. It was a good life together on the farm, never easy, but always we had enough. When Frank gets married and goes off to his own place I will be alone here for the first time.

Your Pa, B.F. Barnett

Franklin
January 31, 1906

Children,

Today I walked down the road and it made me lonesome. I used to see Mama on it when she was young and I could see her as she used to be but alas she is gone never to return here.

The country has made great changes since I was young. I cannot begin to take stock of the automobiles and flying machines, telephones & electric light, and a hundred other wonders.

Land that was not worth more than fifteen dollars an acre now is all ditched out and worth $100 per acre. Was over to our relations place, Joseph Riggs. He has 9 children, one boy by his first wife, 8 by this wife, 6 girls and 2 boys in the last gang. It made me think when we had that many nice behaved children.

All here are well as common far as I know.
B.F. Barnett

Kelley Lake
August 4, 1905

Mr. Nelson,

We understand there is talk of another school closer to Tamarack. We hope it goes in by next year as the No. 69 school is a good long walk. Our daughter Erline is of school age and little Kai soon will be.

Watson Norton Kelley

Duluth Presbytery
February 11, 1906

Friend Marcus,

I am appointing Mamie Superintendent of the Tamarack Sunday School.   I believe that you will approve as Mamie is no longer working in the store and her duties will not conflict with child rearing. I give her full authority to select teachers, implement the curriculum, and encourage attendance. Be good enough to relay the good news.

Pat Barott's have offered their home in town as a regular sunday school but I have high hopes we can raise up a church this summer. We can, of course, take advantage of the Barott's kind offer until then.

Bro. Jameson will be out Sunday next.
With all God's grace, Sam Blair

Friestad's
May 2, 1906

Brother,

The men have finally decided to build a school at Tamarack. About time, as the young ones are wearing out walking to No. 69 or Nelson Lake schools.

John King allowed he would give up a corner of his place, about a mile south of town. H.J. is coming in tomorrow to order lumber. I am to write Mr. J.J. Gildersleeve, Aitkin County School Superintendent, to get things in order and find a teacher for next fall. We expect about 15 pupils to start.

Don't give Anker but one treat for bringing this in and use the 10 lb. jar of butter he brought as trade for a can of Arbuckle coffee, the kind with premiums packed inside.

Emma

36

Minnehaha Falls.

Mpls
July 13, 1906

Husband,

Tingdale's took Myrtle and me to a Chautauqua out at Minnehaha Falls, my first time to one. Had a big tent with all kind of things going on. One fellow gave a lecture on success through positive thinking, a English dandy read from what I suppose was a Shakespeer play and I did not understand a word he said. There was a concert that played popular tunes, followed by jugglers and acrobats, then more lecture and humor men. One fellow could talk faster than any I ever heard. Called himself "Gatling Gun" Fogleman. ha! At the end there was a temperance sermon in which the speaker said "Old Man Barleycorn proves too much for most who tackle him." So true, I could think of any number that got bested.

Was upwards of five thousand that came. They go to Milwaukee next.

Mamie

Tamarack
July 29, 1906

C/O Metropole Hotel, Duluth
Husband,

You had no more than left on the train when Brother Blair fell. He paid no heed to Fred's warning not to go too high on the frame and lost his balance. I got the bones back in under the skin, set & splinted his leg and stopped the bleeding, but he was bad hurt. Mr. Kelley and Mr. Cayo brought him over to Barott's house where he took a fever in the evening but seems to have come out of it today.

I hope this will not hold up the building of the church. I had to get after the men before they would go back to work.

Sam's life is not at risk, Marcus, but I fear for permanent damage. Am sorry as I know how much you think of him. He is a good man and God will have mercy I am sure.

Mamie

LaPorte, Minn.
Dec. 10, 1906

Sister & family,

Well, we Crandalls have decided to stay in Minnesota but hope to move back east someday. John is doing most of the work in the store himself now as trade is not so heavy this winter, no big camps at all. The wood here is thinning out.

The "Lazy" Aid had a Sale and free lunch last Fri. night. Took in $26 but had some expense so will be something over $20 to go toward pastor's

salary. They had two fish ponds for the smaller articles, a 5 cent & 10 cent pond. Had 4 quilts. I did not get to go as it was so stormy.

Have I written since we dedicated our church? I believe you wrote me you were going to dedicate the church there. Have they affected an organization yet?

Your sister, Ida Barnett Crandall

P.S. The neighbor boy has got his foot in it by getting a girl who worked for them in a family way. She just owned to it Sunday. Her folks are nice people & feel so bad. They are going to try to make him suffer for it.

Tamarack
2 P.M. on 3/19/07

M. Nelson C/O St. James Hotel, Mpls
Brother,

I am sitting on a depot bench next to a warm stove watching Mr. Rowbottom telegraph the news to you of your new baby. Mamie tells me a name had already been decided upon, so I expect he is to be Orvis Marcus Nelson.

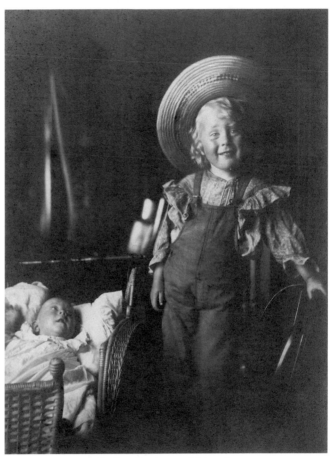

Baby Orvis and Myrtle.

The stork outfoxed you after all. Early last evening Mamie said it was time to put her to bed and had the child about dawn. I do not know why they always want to come then. I, Mrs. Rowbottom, and Mrs. Paxson were with her all night, with Annie Nelson coming upstairs about 4 a.m. There was more that offered but they would have been underfoot.

The baby is healthy & alert with a strong voice. Finish your business and get on home as Mamie felt bad you were not with her again.

Emma

Duluth Presbytery
March 24, 1907

Friend Marcus,

It is pleasing to know that all my very good friends in Tamarack have not forgotten me. Brother Jameson brought the kindly envelope of money for which I am most grateful. I am pleased the Presbyterian Church of Tamarack membership is growing and that I may have left some little mark of good.

The doctor tells me I should expect my leg not to get any better. I can get around O.K. on a castered office chair and my heart and lungs are tolerably well, so I hope to still be able to do useful work in this world.

My studies progress satisfactorily and I soon hope to be ordained.

Please do come see me next chance you get.
Sam Blair

Orvis and little friends.

Fred Nelson children; (L to R) Ernest, Maurice (pronounced Morris) and Alice.

Kelley Lake
May 14, 1907

Dear Uncle Marcus and Aunt Mamie,

Thank you for inviting me to Myrtle birthday party. Pa says tell you my sisters Kai and Laurilee say thank you to. It was a verry good chocolate cake and iceing.

Say hello to Paxsons and to Alice and Ernest and little Maurice Nelson. Are they staying over nite with you?

Baby Orvis verry pretty. I will be 11 yrs old next July 15 and I wish school would start again so I can see all my Tamarack friends ever day.
Erline Kelley

"ROUND LAKE" TAMARACK. MINN
FAMOUS BASS LAKE

V-214

Tingdale Bros.
Mpls
July-7-07

Dear Moxie,

Say old boy, can you tell me in a few short words how fishing is this year? Is John Anderson still up at Round Lake? That is such a good fishing lake I would not want to go up there without trying it again for a day. Last year the black bass were falling all over themselves to bite.

Let me know a little about these things as brother Martin and I are counting on sneaking out of town for a few days and drowning some bait up in the same good old place.

Can your road up there be traveled by horses now?

Rudy Tingdale

Jay Lake
April 25th, '08

Marcus,

Well, I have decided to pull out. No use to try and talk me out of it - you have done your best but it won't wash.

Marcus, you know I am a solitary man. If I am around too many folks for too long I get to feeling boxed in. I have always been more comfortable in the forest surrounded by all God's creations.

When I came to this country there were no white men, unless you count old Bill Horn up to Sandy. He was a crazy old man, the Indians were deathly afraid of him and never went near his place on the deep bay.

I can remember canoeing around Sandy and the thick forest canopy would droop out over the lake and you could boat along the shore in the shade. The dam changed all that, the trees by the edge of the water have had the ground washed out from under them and are gone. Here at Tamarack there are four passenger trains and God alone knows how many freights screaming through day and night. It's too much for an old hermit like me.

John Maxwell wrote I could come live with him on the White Earth Reservation over to Detroit City and that is where I will go. I shall raise my bees and hunt and fish as long as I hold out. But don't worry, your faithful friend and Uncle will come back and visit often.

Jay B. Clark

Mpls
May Second, '08

Brother,

We will take the train up around the 25th and hope to stay a week. Warren and Mildred are very excited about tenting at your Round Lake place. Fred said he has never seen a clearer lake, such fine sand beaches and gentle slopes into the water, all spring fed. He claims you can actually see the fish bite your worm!

Josie

Willard Hotel
Aitkin
May 8, 1908

Marcus,

The wife writes the boys are raising money to get up a town baseball team and that you are holding the tin cup. Put the Sandy River Lbr. Co. down for $5 and I will tell her to run the money over.

I have Myrtle's birthday present in hand and will be back to Tamarack in plenty of time to get it to Mamie for wrapping. It is a wonderfully pretty doll whose eyes roll closed when you lay her down and whose hair looks to be real. I have not seen the like - I wonder where Potter-Casey got it?

Ed Douglas

Balsam Town
May 23, -08

Mr. Nelson -

You had ought to know what has become of that Mr. Oberheim whose claim you helped find up to Savanna Lake. He had been living at the John Larsen's while building his cabin. The other night a hoot owl called and the gentleman sat up the rest of the night to repel the invaders. In the morning he went back to Larsen's. They had quite a time laughing at him so he decided to go back that night. On his way over a big gray wolf contested his right-of-way. After dark a Porky Pine called and started to chew on his door and Mr. Oberheim proceeded to shoot the corner of his door off. The next day he stopped at Larsen's to pick up his stuff, told what had happened, and lit out for we know not where.

Mrs. H. Deremo

Mpls
June Third, '08

Brother,

O such a fine time with you folks on Round Lake! Who would think a hundred and fifty miles from the hot and dirty city would make such a difference - the sweet smelling evergreens, fresh cool air - and oh yes all the quiet. We could just "hear" the quiet. It seems to me there must be some money to be made promoting such a healthful place as a vacation destination.

It was fun having you men catch fish and make breakfast before we ladies got up, then shoot some ducks when it was supper time. Foods tastes ever so much better over a camp fire. And what a sight that was when our driving rigs moved up and down the sandy shores with ribbons billowing and bells jingling. It was as if we were Royalty touring our own private Kingdom!

Mildred & Warren are still talking about when Uncle Fred decided to show off and jumped on a pony and rode into the lake where the water was quite deep. I laughed so when the horse sagged and Fred slid into the water and got waterlogged. The best was when Mamie came up with a pair of her bloomers for him to wear home. He didn't look too bad in them. Ha! Ha!

Josie

Camping at Round Lake

*Myrtle on pony, Paul Heller next to Marcus,
and the Mapes family join the Nelsons.*

*As usual, Marcus is the
camp cook.*

*Assorted Friestads, Andersons, Tingdales, and Nelsons. Grandma Nielsen
and Josie in middle back. Fred (suspenders) and Annie under clothesline.*

Sandy River Lumber Company Tamarack
June 11, '08

Marcus,

I about ran back to my store office as I could not wait to write you to Cloquet and tell what happened. Mamie is the dangdest woman I ever knew. A man could not put one over on her anymore than you can catch a weasel asleep.

That Jew trader E.Z. Mark (which he is not) got into town this morning to run a horse sale at the depot corral. He got Martin Newstrom from over to Aitkin to cry the auction and started right up.

The sale wasn't doing too good so old Mark determined to pep things up with an offer to give away a free horse to anyone who could ride it. Out comes this big snake-eyed roan, pawing, snorting, and foaming at the mouth and brisket. The crowd was sitting on the top rail of the corral waiting for a volunteer but no one came forward.

Old Mark, rubbing his hands now that he had everyone's attention, started to run at the mouth trying to goad somebody into taking the matter up. Finally a voice calls out, "Why don't you ask Marcus' wife?" E.Z. chuckles long and deep, then walks over & dares Mamie to make the ride.

About this time I held up my hand and said, "Why now, it ought to be worth more for a woman to try and ride that kind of animal." Mark looks in my direction, one eye squinted shut from the sun, and says, "What is it you have in mind Douglas?" I cleared my throat, noticing the crowd was hanging on every word. "Ride like that," I says, "ought to be worth the roan and another $10.00 to boot." Mark lets go with a big haw, haw and says, "Sir, let us make it $20.00 gold coin, for I do

Tamarack corral. Douglas' store was behind tarpapered barn.

43

not think you have a rider in this half horse town, male or female, who can stay with my horse." "Done," I says, ignoring the insult and not quite sure what had gotten into me.

E.Z. walks over to Mamie and says, "What about it madam, or are you only for show?" Mamie got that look in her eye that I hope never gets aimed in my direction and jumped down into the corral yelling, "Saddle him up!"

Your wife rode down to the sale and had on her homemade split skirt riding outfit so she was ready to go before the horse was. While the womenfolk gasped, Charley Anderson threw her up by the knee and the show was on. I have never seen a woman look so sure on a bronc and cannot begin to explain how she stayed on but before anyone knew it she had rode him to a standstill. The whole town broke into a cheer. Folks are in my store right now still talking abut it. 'Ol Mark is down at the depot sitting on his grip, counting the minutes till the train comes.

One thing I forgot to say. When E.Z. handed over the double eagle, Mamie walked the roan up to us and said in a loud voice, "Ed, do we have enough yet to build the church parsonage?" That's what really done that Jew in. I am laughing so hard, I need to quit.

E.F. Douglas

Haugen Township
Aug. 15, '08

Mr. Nelson,

Glory Be! The road from Tamarack has finally reached us. No more tethering teams at the big hill, skinning logs to town, and all the rest.

They were laying 8-foot wide tamarack corduroy for weeks. They'd have her built up high at nightfall but by morning the whole pile had sunk into the swamp, then they'd have to do her all over again the next day.

Graders and gravel haulers are still running back and forth in front of the place as they work their way north. There is a big cloud of dust that sits over the farm 24 hours a day but we do not mind in the least for at last we can take the rig all the way to town. I've heard they have cut south of

Tamarack past the school and beyond, and that now you can drive out as far as your folk's lake.

I think, Marcus, your efforts with the political men have helped bring this along and everyone is grateful to you and Commissioner Odegard, who finally got something away from Aitkin.

F.J. Fahrwald

Friestad's
Sept. 24th, '08

Brother,

I must tell you the story Myrtle told us last night. I do not know if it is so or another of your tales but, anyway, Myrtle says you were tenting at the mouth of Prairie River near where you aim to put up a drive camp. Now I'm reading between the lines for Myrtle got so excited it came out a jumble, but she said that along about dark 2 birch bark canoes full of Indians landed on the sand bar and invited themselves over to the fire, took supper, and that you stayed up to all hours telling them stories. Myrtle said she was so scared she could not go to bed for fear they would scalp her while she slept but that Mamie took the baby and went to sleep in the tent. Myrtle woke up in the morning wondering how she got inside and when she peaked under the flap the Indians were gone and you were making breakfast.

Emma

The tent was on the foreground, left side.

44

Mpls
Dec 4 '08

Son Marcus,

Your letter of Superior in hand. i am sory last letter went in Norwegian. as i get old i forget.

I am glad to hear you are out on business. wi are glad Every Time wi get a letter from you. Special wen it sound prosperity.

In regard to man renting he is the begeste liar i ever know and im sory that a so big wreck is on mi place. that is wat i say and i belief he crack off a lie every time he open his mouth. you kan tel him that. not more this time -

My head wass better on the cold days dan it is today.

Well, God By

Yours truly, Fader

P.S. Mama is as ordinary

Edinburg, Ind.
Mar. 30, 1909

Sister & family,

Deocia wrote that Marcus don't want to live in Fred's house in town anymore and was talking about building a new place on the rise east of Tamarack. When would he start on the work?

How big is Myrtle & brother? Suppose she thinks she can wash dishes. Zelma got the Xmas card from her. She has a big album she puts all the postals in.

Suppose Marcus is stouter than he was. Travis is coming after him in height Marcus are you not six feet and two inches? Zelma is not as tall as I am and likely won't be as none of us Barnett women ever reach over five and a half feet.

Come out and help selebrate our "china wedding" next Aug. You had the "tin wedding" for us. Them was gay old times.

Sister Maggie Nay

Haugen Township
April 18th, 1909

Marcus,

Enclosed find the plans for your fine new house. There will be 4 bedrooms, 3 upstairs and 1 down. On the first floor is a large kitchen, pantry, dining room, parlor with fireplace, and a full front porch facing west. The second floor will be dormered out on 3 sides so that we may put in big vertical windows for extra light and also provide more standing room in the bedrooms.

The basement will be full, with a large wood or coal burning boiler and tin pipes built inside the walls to carry the heat throughout the whole house. The rest of the basement can be used as a vegetable cellar, laundry, and wood storage.

I think you are wise to insist on running water, under pressure. This will allow us to include a water closet, something only the best city homes

have. A nice heated bath-room with bath-tub and wash-sink can also be built next to the water closet. I have been studying Modern Plumbing for some time and am glad for the chance to do some actual work. Remind me to explain about stench traps, waste piping, drainage, and the like. Care must be used to avoid odors, contamination, and disease.

Regards the water pressure problem, we will install a large water tank in the walk-in attic, which can be supplied by either hand pumping water up to it or by a Fairbanks or Morse Gasoline Engine.

We can also construct a pipe to receive rain water from off the eaves-troughs. With water above the plumbing, there will be pressure enough to operate the water closet. Heat from the furnace will make hot water in a large Copper Boiler, so that you may have both hot & cold running water to the bathroom, kitchen, and laundry.

City homes are being built with electric lines and I can run these behind the wall lath. It may be some time before you can get the electric but when that day comes you will be the cock of the walk.

Carl Odegard

Trafalgar, Ind.
July 26th, 1909

Sister,

I was surprised when I heard of your going to have an operation. I didn't know that there was anything so severe as that. Yes, I have heard of the great success of the Rochester Hospital and sincerely hope you will soon be feeling all right again.

Your children are harty looking in the pictures you sent. Orvis is a fat little fellow and Myrtle looks like a real little lady. Are those Ole's girls? They are all grown up now.

Well, I will write to the others that I can't see to let read your letter. Take the best of care of yourself.

Your Affectionate Sister, Cora Musselman
P.S. I know you are unhappy you have been unable to get Marcus to confess Christ but the Lord moves in misterious ways and you should not lose heart but let Him work His wonders.

Richmond, Va.
July 29, 1909

My Dear Sister Mamie,

We had a letter from Marcus in which he said the operation was over & you were doing well. He said the Dr. was mistaken about it being a cancer. I was so glad to hear that, for one never knows what will be the result of cancer cures. However, I know it was nothing easy to place one's self in the hands of strange Doctors & Nurses for such an ordeal. If one knew they were conscientious Christian people, it is not so bad, but it is only the grace of God that can carry one over such hard places. I have been praying for you & the loved one's left at home without you, and shall continue to do so. It is my earnest prayer that he may restore you to health & strength and spare you many, many years for the useful life you are living in His service. God bless you, my dear.

Lovingly,
Ida Crandall

Tamarack
Aug. 3rd, 1909

Husband,

You got in so late last night & left for Aitkin so early this morning I did not get the chance I wanted to talk to you.

I opened that envelope for Myrtle by mistake, thinking it was for me. I was so sorry on account of the pleasure it would have given her to open it herself. But she had a big smile when she pulled out the Ribbon.

Orvis has been talking all the time past few days, his favorite words are "hello there." He is a good boy. They both have been sleeping well, so they get up rested in the morning.

I will make fried chicken for supper day after tomorrow so do not fail to come home.

Mamie

Mpls
Aug 30, 1909

Brother & family,

Martin, I, and children had a grand time at your Saturday barn raising. Scores of men and their families come to your place and in one day put up the whole skeleton of a barn! Martin said those tamarack timbers were near a foot thick and weigh hundreds of pounds each. He reckoned it was the

biggest barn in your part of the country. Is that what they call a Gambrel style roof? The two cupolas will look as big as some houses we have seen!

Good to see Mamie well & her old self, bossing the camp cooks and so on. Mr. Lang jumped every time she looked his way. That was some job in the back yard of roasting all that beef on spits. And the kettles and pans of soups, beans, potatoes, sweet breads, and pies cooking over open fires made everybody's mouth water until they couldn't stand it.

I enjoyed listening to the ladies talk about Tamarack. They surely feel it is their town and will stick up for it at every turn.

Did you see Warren, Mildred, Myrtle, Orvis, and all the other little ones sitting on the lumber piles with their mouths agape at all the doings? The men puffed up and talked louder whenever the children were near, and of course the tales got taller with all those little saucer eyes boring in on the spinner.

But the high point of the day was when the men shouldered their pike poles and tugged at the pulleys to raise up one at a time all five framing sections. Warren said the men scurrying across the top to tie everything together looked like "monkeys." Land sakes they could scat! I'll bet there was some tired folks that night but they looked happy and I guess they know their own turn will come.

Josie

P.S. Martin believes your big new house is a fine work and says will last for a hundred years. The Vanderbilts ought to pay a call and see how it is done.

Haugen Town
Oct. 25, 1909

Sir:

We will blow stumps and grub out the road on the 3/4 mile north of Tamarack River according to specifications for the sum of $240.00. Also the 1/2 mile north of Sections 3-4-9-10, Town of Haugen, for the sum of $160.00. Road to link up with corduroy road to Tamarack. Who is to build the bridge over Tamarack River?

Andrew Olson

Tamarack
Nov 15, '09

M. Nelson
    West Superior Hotel, Wisc.
Husband,
    The State Welfare is of the opinion that not only would the store hire young Gust Oja but that you had agreed to take the orphan in. He is but 11 years old and we can only hope this does not prove to be too much for us. Expect we will find out soon enough as last night he came over from Wright having walked the track the full six miles in the rain before losing his nerve & hiding in the barn.

    I went out there on account my new ponies were nickering and I was fearful of a wolf or bear. I opened the door and there stood Gust shivering and soaked to skin, pale as a ghost. He was holding a gun and I asked what he was doing out there as did not recognize him. He said had come to see Mr. Nelson then I knew who he was but that he had gotten afraid and went in the barn out of the rain. I looked back at the gun and asked if it was loaded. He said no but as his English is so poor I did not trust his answer. I made him

break it open and there was a shell. I must have looked awful cross because he begun to cry and babble in Finn then handed me the gun. Later he told me he did not think a gun loaded till cocked!
    I rushed the boy into the house and got him into dry clothes, fed some broth, and put him to bed as he was coming down with something. Looks better this morning but nervous. Will keep him in bed today and then if fit will take down to store tomorrow morning and have Herb put him to work.
    Mamie

Emerald Grove Stock Farm
Janesville, Wisc.
Jan. 27, 1910

Nelson Pony Farm
    Tamarack, Minn.
Mrs. Mamie Nelson:
    Yours received in regard to purchasing more Shetland Stallions. The price I have is from 100 to 150 dollars per head. They are of all colors, there are a good many bays and blacks among them. If you send me the exact height and color of the pony you want to pair up I could match it.
    For the past 3 years I have sold all my filly colts when they were from 8 to 12 months old for 100 dollars. As you know there are not much sale for horse colts until they are 2 years old. I do not sell any ponies for less than 100 dollars.
    You are getting into this business at a good time as the demand for ponies is still increasing. I have done very well.
    Robert Lilburn

NELSON PONY FARM

Registered Shetland Ponies
Silver Tipped Wyandotte Chickens

Mamie B. Nelson

Tamarack, Minn,, *March 2²* 191_

Kelley Lake
May 19th, -10

Mr. and Mrs. Nelson,

   Our daughter Erline, along with Master Allison Paxson, will graduate from the 8th Grade on Sunday, May 22nd, instant. This is the first class in Tamarack to graduate. Mr. E.H. Hall, County Superintendent, will be present at the King School to pass out the diplomas and honor us with a few remarks.

   We wish you would come at 2:00PM and there will be a little lunch afterward. Bring Myrtle and Orvis too.

   Mr. and Mrs. W.N. Kelley

Main Drive Camp
Sandy Lake
July 14th, 1910

Husband,

   Lake life is agreeable and Arthur Lang has cooked up some fine meals. Believe he enjoys the children and having a lively dinner for a change instead of having to feed smelly old men all winter.

   I see there are 3 or 4 crippled 'jacks sponging off his table supposedly they are to see to stock and buildings but are of little account. Hope you not paying them much as are losing money.

   Fred came at noon with Kelley girls, the three little Friestads, Paxsons, and his own kids. We decided to stay in the cook shanty as Lang keeps the stove hot & evenings get chilly. After dinner I made children rest for an hour so they would not get cramps before running over the hill to the lake to go swimming. Indian Charlie and Fred are looking after them.

Sandy Lake bathing beauties.

49

Most of the Friestads. Helga stands next to her father.

Myrtle and Orvis were glad to get company. Yesterday the two of them went wading in the Prairie River after I told them not to and proceeded to fill up on blood suckers. Had a time getting the things off what with all the caterwauling, esp. poor Orvis. He had one stuck between his toes. Scared the pants off him when it broke and bled on his foot.

Lang found 3 bee trees. Have two of them but one we will leave in the woods and rob this fall.

Mamie

P.S. Oughten we buy this place? It's very restful here.

Tamarack
10/2/10

Mr. Nelson,

I come from Wayzata, Minn. and have taken a homestead near Kelley Lake but there is not enough to live on. Word is you are looking for a barn man at your farm. I have done that line of work and would ask for the job. I can start in right away.

Dennis A. Carr

Studebaker Bros. Mpls
Oct. 4, 1910

Mr. Nelson:
    We are shipping in 3 or 4 days your order for a #646 Shetland Pony harness for children's cart. We can assure Mrs. Nelson our harnesses are of the very best quality and she need have no fear of failure that would do injury to her children.
    Studebaker of Minn.

Orvis and Myrtle in front of Nelson's store.

Every pony was a pet.

Tamarac
Fri Oct 14 of 10

Mr. Nelson Sir:

I respectedly ask fur 2 days a way frum store 2 goe hunting Mrs. Nelson a deer and other game for her smokhaus & pan tree. Sir, do i hav 2 goe 2 skul on munday?

Yours verry respectedly,

Gust Oja

Peterson-Retrum Battery Co.
Dawson, Minn.
Dec. 19/1910

Mr. Markus Nelson:-

I enclose literature regarding an electric plant for your farm. We claim we have the only electric plant for farm purposes that is manufactured today. Ours have stood the test, and is past experimental stages. Our men is at present putting in a plant for the Lac Qui Parle County Poor Farm. This shows up good for our plants as they have been looking over several kinds of lighting systems but have found nothing to take the place of ours.

C.C. Retrum, Sec'y

How does Myrtle like her first months at the King School? I suppose she is old enough to walk by herself.

I suppose you have had sleigh rides before this. Good night.

Your Pa, B.F. Barnett

P.S. I will send a dollar in paper for Xmas.

Franklin
Dec. 22, 1910

Children,

Received the family picture. You look thinner, Mamie, than you were when last I saw you. Daisy wants to know how Marcus got the curl out of his hair. Marcus, I noticed you looked a little different but did not know just what it was until she spoke about your hair.

Nelson Pony Farm
Monday, Jan 9th, '11

M. Nelson C/O Willard Hotel, Aitkin
Husband,

Myrtle, Orvis, Gust, and I took up your offer to visit the Savanna River Camp. Dennis Carr drove us out Sat. morning. We had fun except Myrtle's jaw ached in the cold, appears to be getting worse again. Lang asked me to do a Bible reading before Sunday dinner and the boys said they enjoyed it.

Left camp at 4 PM Sunday, drove down the river, and bucked our way up the bank at the drive camp. By then the children were getting cold and was dark so Carr bundled them up with wool blankets in the back of the sleigh. Drove home by star light. Calm and clear the air so crispy cold our noses & cheeks tingled. Only thing we could hear was jangling of sleigh bells and crunch of horse hooves in the snow. A big old gray wolf followed a while but lost interest when he learned he would get nothing for his trouble.

Mr. Carr feel asleep before we got to town but the team knew the way so did not have to wrestle away the reins. The children were dead tired and had to carry them into house. I gave Dennis a cup of coffee and a slice of pie after he put horses up and started a fire in his little house. He is good to the children and like the grandfather they never see. Too bad both live so far away.

Mamie

Trafalgar, Ind.
June 29th, 1911

Sister,

How do you like this post card of Mr. Musselman's prize Saddle Mare? He is awful proud of his stock. How are your Ponys and Colts getting along?

Mamie, someone was telling me that you fell down the basement steps & cut your head & was unconscious for awhile.

How are the children and did they get the little trinkets I sent them, beads & little hand pocket?

Cora Musselman

Mamie at the reins.

53

Nelson Pony Farm
Aug. 11th, '11

Paris Hotel, Benson, Minn.
Husband,

Had a bad storm last evening after supper and lighting hit the fence killed two of my ponies. They were leaning against the wire when it hit. I heard the boom and then herd stampeded and when I went to see I found 2 of them burnt up. Silver Heels and Tiny Delos.

We had only just broke Tiny to Myrtle's little cart. She been crying all morning and I cannot get her to stop. Orvis been with her giving little pats to try and make her stop. O. been brave and acts like man of family with you off again and Carr down to his place grubbing stumps and haying.

Well, you should know there is lots of equipment coming through town to build the Black Diamond Trail, will be a real improvement over the snakey tote ruts. Have finished between here and McGregor and now will build up the road north of Tamarack about 2 miles, then cut east to Wright, Cromwell, and on to Carlton. Looks like won't be long before we will be able to take a rig all the way to Duluth. Roads have gotten easier to come by in this country what with the better drainage.

Glad you sold 5 carloads of lumber but when can you come home? I wish I was alone with you, etc.

Mamie

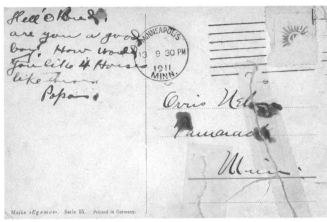

Hell'o Bud.
are you a good
boy! How would
you like 4 Horses
like these.
            Papa.

Nelson Pony Farm
May 10th, 1912

Dear Papa,
Please read this story called The Lion And The Mouse -

Once upon a time there was a lion and a mouse. The lion had sharp claws and soft paws and long teeth.

The lion caught a mouse.

The mouse begged the lion to let go. He said O King of Beasts let me go. I will do you a favor.

And the lion said you may go but you are too little to do a favor for me.

One day not long after the mouse heard the lion roar. He ran as fast as he could to see what was the matter.

There lay the King of Beasts in a hunters net, held fast by strong cords.

And the mouse said I have come to help you. You were kind to me and now I will help you in your trouble.

Then he cut the cords with his teeth and set the lion free. He said you once thought that I was too little to do you a favor but you have found that it is well to have a friend even among the little people.

The End
By Myrtle Nelson

54

Niels Nielsen
Mpls 5/12/12

Dear Folks,
This was taken this
spring. Kids are racing
home from town. Myrtle
is better again. Feels
pretty good now.
Much love,
Mamie Nelson

Nelson Pony Farm
May 14, 1912

C/O Tingdale Bros., Mpls
Husband,

Made a day of it yesterday went to Rice Lake to celebrate Myrtle's 8th and Magdalene Friestad's 13th birthday. I organized a hay ride for a gang and Kai Kelley drove their team of mules. We went all the way to end of point at Chas. Wiberg's old place, where you and Martin are talking about putting up vacation cottages. The pine is coming back fine there, makes it look pleasing, the trees alongside the lake.

I served a big lunch and did those young folks wolf it down. Was nary a scrap left. Everyone had fun but there was a number of them that could not keep their eyes open on the way home and fell asleep in the hay.

Got 1912 tax bill of Fred. Being the brother of Clark Township assessor has done you no good.

Have put in flowers all around the house - hollyhocks, marigolds, dahlias, tiger lilies, etc. Looks nice.

Mamie

P.S. Was looking at that picture of Carr deviling cats I made last winter. Have a notion to make it into a xmas postcard.

Nelson Pony Farm
Oct. 2, 1912

Stratton House, Brainerd
Husband,

Our dear, suffering little dog Topsy passed away yesterday, aged 11 years 11 months. The children been in a constant state of mourning since.

Held a funeral service on the porch and laid her to rest in the flower bed in front of the house. Orvis says we must work up a marker so I am to make a mold & we will use concrete to form a headstone with writing on it. Dog had been with me since I lived in section house with Deocia.

The men got together and chased off that band of gypsies camped down to Sandy River. Too much livestock been walking off and came to head when Douglas caught one stealing in his store.

Mamie

Hornbrook, Calif.
Dec. 16, 1912

Sister,

Received the Christmas bill and found they had sent 1 doz. handkerchiefs to you. So if Myrtle received one dozen, I will send you stamps to send 1/2 doz. to Kate's children as they are going to school they can make use of a good many.

How does Fred and Annie get along? Does her brother Charley Anderson still log for Marcus? Tamarack has had many new buildings put up since we were there.

Did Marcus vote for Taft or Teddy? Ed voted for Teddy and lost his vote. He had half a notion to vote for Wilson but was a little afraid of hard times.

Deocia Lilliedale

Nelson Pony Farm
3/26/13

C/O Niels Nielsen, Mpls
Husband,

Forgot to tell you be sure and go to Dr. about your throat. Also get lungs and spitum examined so as to know for sure if you have any bugs.

Herb Colmer just telephoned from store for your heavy coat. Did not say what he wanted it

Nomads catching the next freight out of Tamarack.

for. He claims Douglas or Creamery always pick up when he calls out here. It is because he is careless way he cranks and does not get the one long and two short way he should.

Hope all well with old folks. Myrtle sends a card.

Mamie

Papa,

How are you I am fine. Mama had her camera on stilts and I got on a box & looked under the black cloth through the glass & everything was upside down. Looked funny. I will close for this time.

Yours lovingly, Myrtle Nelson

way to town and we want everyone to get all decked out.

Well, I expect you heard they have hired me and my boy Percy to build a bridge over the Prairie River next to your drive camp. The end of ferry crossings will be a boon to all. I need more men, can you spare any? I hired Elmer LeVesseur and his big team to haul.

After the bridge is raised, they will build a good road on the north side of the river up to all the new settlements everyone seems to believe will be coming in. My daughter Elise got it into her head to homestead up that way, on the north side of Sandy. Calls the place Pine Beach, for that is what it surely is. She believes it is better to own lake shore than farm land in this country. Well, at least with my bridge you will be able to get a rig or even an automobile up to her claim. Bye the bye, Mr. LeVesseur has asked to call on her.

Joe Cayo

Mrs. Odegard leads parade over N.P. tracks.

Zion's Hill
July 1, 1913

Marcus,

Just about the whole country is coming to the 4th of July. This will be the biggest celebration we've ever had. We have the bowery about set up in that lot by the Tamarack Presbyterian Church. Phil and Pat Barott will be on the violin and their wives will play guitar. I am to call as usual. Everyone is to gather at Barott's place on Round Lake in the morning and there will be a big parade all the

Float passing tracks, depot on left.

57

Sandy River Lumber Co.
Aug. 21st, 1913

Bridge over Prairie River.

Marcus,

The new school is ready for the term to start, approved for grades 1-4 in the lower room and 5-8 in the upper. We plan a ceremony Sat. noon to officially open Tamarack School District #53, and so of course be sure you are not out of town. The big new building is a fine addition to the community and should be more than adequate for our growing crop of youngsters for years to come.

Everything is moved from the King School and the building is empty. Col. King said he will tear it down for the lumber.

Ed Douglas

Fergus Falls, Minn.
Nov 7, '13

Mrs. Nelson -

Yes we got the pony O.K. and are very pleased with him. When we have a picture of him taken we will send you one and if you ever want any refference those who send me a stamp for returns I will give a good word tords your ponys as he is just what you said he was.

Our boy is 9 years old and has it 2 miles to school and that is what I got the pony for him to go to school with. I can ashure you to rest at ease that the pony has a good home & Georgie loves him & won't drive him too hard.

Mrs. H.G. Oleitz

Trafalgar, Ind.
Jan 28 - 1914

Sister & family,

The last two weeks I have been studying on my part in a play we are going to give on Valentine's night. There are thirteen in it, all married except four young girls. We will give it in the hall and the proceeds will go to the Christian Church.

Here is a picture that was taken last summer of a play we gave where three of the women dressed in men's clothes. Another was blacked up to represent a colored servant. See if you can tell which one is me.

Daisy is the policeman on the left.

The play was where two toughs drag a nice young man down to drinking & gambling and his sister, mother, and sweet heart were so worried but did not know how to save him. An old Aunt comes to visit and they tell her of it and after the others go to bed the Aunt gets that colored servant to help her and they make a raid and find the boy drunk and in these other two boys come, so they call the police and have them taken to jail. Those two women with those long coats on are the police. We had a platform fixed up in front of Mr. Gashwiller's house and lanterns hung out on the lawn where the audience set.

Dilla's Johnny is wearing long pants now. Makes him look larger.

Daisy

P.S. Pa went up to Indianapolis to see the President on the 9th of Jan. First time he had ever seen one. Said was hard work, such a big crowd.

Tingdale Bros. Realty, Mpls
May 21st, 1914

Marcus,

Received a surprise card from Orvis. He says what he likes best about school was intermission when they conduct sling shot fights in the woods and play pom pom pullaway in the yard. He asked for a job "selling real states." He is alert for so young, does Mamie give home lessons on top of school?

Martin

Nelson Pony Farm
May 25, 1914

C/O Maddy Hotel, McGregor
Husband,

School is over and we have got the children's final report cards. They both passed to the next level.

Orvis, Maurice, and Ernest Nelson have been knuckling down on the drive way all morning & into the afternoon. Are play "mibs," as they call it. Orvis whispered to me at dinner was 40 ahead, including a "rubie," a "aggie," 2 I think "steelies" and one other kind I didn't catch maybe was "milkie." Funny names. ha. They are playing for Keeps and so of course this is a grim day of business.

Mamie

P.S. The feed mill rats are big as beavers. Can you not get Gust O. to trap them out before they ruin you.

Nelson's Store
June 6th, 1914

J.B. Lemire, Aitkin County Auditor
Sir:-

Please send me a plank County Road Petetion. by return Mail. Sorry new typewriter.

Marcus Nelson

Reply -

Marcus, I have no plank road petitions. Use this one.

J.B.

Tingdale Bros., Mpls
Oct 1, 1914

Marcus:-

Josie informs me Mamie had to sew 12 stitches into Orvis' head after he fell off the school bell porch and landed on the front steps. Hope Myrtle is still not so upset over all the blood, head wounds are like that. That boy is quite a caution, expect his Father tanned his britches to even out the discomfort.

Martin

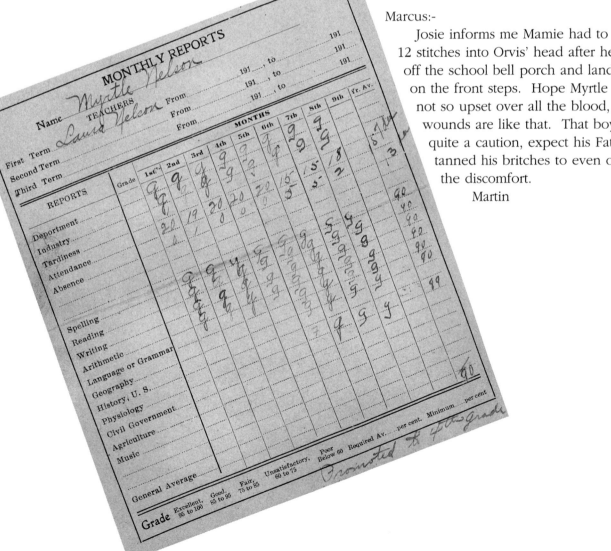

Nelson Pony Farm
Oct 29, 14

Papa,
    I wrote a poem for school here it is -
      "IF I HAD A HOLIDAY THIS P.M"
    I would go home as fast as I could.
    Help Mama wash the dinner dishes.
        Put up the ponies.
     Swing on our new swing.
        Help git supper.
   Help wash the supper dishes.
     Clean up my bed room.
     Go out and play again.
       Then go to bed.
           Lovingly, Myrtle Nelson

Nelson Pony Farm
Nov 2, 14

C/O Willard Hotel, Aitkin
Papa,
    On Sat. Orvis, Gust, and me played in the barn & jumped on the hay. Orvis climbed all the way to the top of the hay mow ladder and jumped a hundred feet! Gust bawled him out.

After sunday school Mama took me & Orvis to Sandy Lake. One of your logging Indians brought us to their village and they put on a war dance. Was I ever scared! When can you be allowed to come home?
    Myrtle

Minutes of the Secret Club
Saturday Jan 16th 1915

The members met Secretly in the root cellar next to the coal bin. They gave each other the Secret Sign. The members played house. They then went to see the Nelson's little chickens. They will meet at Paxson's house next time. Had no visitors. All members present. They then went home.
    Myrtle Nelson, Scribe

Nelson Pony Farm
Sat - April - 3 - 1915

Dear Indiana Cousins,
    Elfel, we got your letter. April Fool yourself.
    Papa and Mama are both reading. Orvis wants them to go out on the lawn with him but it's too wet. Snow melting everywhere.
    What did you people get for Christmas? I got a camera, kewpie doll, apron, breakfast cap, 2 handkerchiefs, a pair of finger gloves, and ribbons. Orvis got a moving picture machine, a watch (cheap), a handkerchief, and 2 ties (one from you people).
    I received a song book from Aunt Ida not long ago. It is swetting hot in this room.
    I must close.
    Myrtle Nelson

Prairie River Main Drive Camp
June 13-15

Marcus -

   Mamie, Elise LeVesseur, and Myrtle got here this morning and rowed a boat over to Battle Island to sun bathe and look for arrowheads. Sandy is dead calm.

   Mamie is put out with me that I let Orvis get so dirty. I guess the backs of his ears was a little green but I don't know it hurt him any. He is back out on the river, soaked to the gills, pushing logs here & there, and generally trying to act like a river pig. His mother would have a duck-fit if she saw him.

   "Bud" is good help when I can keep his mind on things, clever with his hands. He sassed me but once and then we had that cleared up. He made a fine sounding slip-whistle from a sappy willow branch and tootles on that when not engaged in his river work.

   The kids asked for a big batch of doughnuts for supper tonight so expect I better get at it.

   A.F. Lang

P.S. As you asked, Indian Charlie is keeping a close eye on Orvis.

Nelson Pony Farm
July 19, 1915

Cousin Mildred,

   Papa took us on a trip to Duluth. Saw millions of automobiles, and tall buildings, and big ships, and everything.

   We saw a play "The Bird of Paradise." The actress was Anna Held. They even had volcanoes & flames but nothing burnt up. Papa liked it very much but Bud only liked when the volcano rupted.

   I sure like it when Papa and Mama take us places. Does Uncle Martin take you places?

   Mildred will you please write to me, now you see, I've written to you.

   Myrtle "Billie" Nelson

2628 W. Lake Street
Mpls
Nov 6, 1915

Cousin "Billie,"

   Please excuse me for not writing but as usual I have been very busy doing nothing. Nothing isn't the right word. I take music lessons and I must practice, and then I have my schoolwork, so I really am quite busy. Do you still take music lessons? I suppose. Do you go to school every day, like I do? I reckon you do.

   I reckon, I reckon. "She's a right smart gal, I reckon." Oh, do you remember, reckon, reckon.

   It's kind of cold here but very lovely. Your father called my father up this afternoon, and I wonder if you and I couldn't of talked just one little minute. But - - -

   Good Bye

   Mildred Tingdale

White Earth Reservation Waubun, Minn.
6/4/16

Miss "Billie" Nelson, Tamarack
Dear Niece,

I should have replied to your letter sooner but have been O so busy. Today is Sunday but I have worked all day (bad old man). I guess I won't have time to be good until I am real old. That will be time enough, don't you think?

I have a nice garden planted. Everything is up and growing except the melons. John Maxwell is all through seeding, except flax, and he will finish that tomorrow. The bees are doing fine, fetching honey in good shape (ask Mr. Rhody at the depot to keep an eye out for an express package).

Tell Mama that bee stings are good for rheumatism. Tell Bud hello, and tell Papa that I never hear a word and don't love him anymore.

Uncle Jay B. Clark

Sandy River Lumber Co.
June 26, 1916

Marcus,

It has been fixed up for next year that Freeman Tweedy will run a "school bus" to the Balsam School. They are so spread out up there and can't allow the little ones to be further exposed to the dark, cold, and wild life. Those big gray wolves will not leave the settlers alone.

This bus is a covered wagon and then he will go to a covered sled with the snow. Tweedy says he will use his team of mules. Mrs. John Larson has been asked to have the foot warming bricks ready each morning.

Ed Douglas

Nelson's Store
June 27, 1916

Willard Hotel, Aitkin
Mr. Nelson,

I have Bud peeling posts and ties in the yard, and will be sure to keep him busy. Fred let him run his skidding team and the boy did not do too bad. There is getting to be a big pile-up at the mill as the sawing can't keep up. Bud is after me to let him operate the mill saw now that you are gone and his mother is out of sight but I will not let him.

Mamie decided to drive herself up to Sandy Lake & fetch that stuff from Lang herself. Said it was bumpy but the car gave no trouble at all. Made a point of telling me she is the first woman to make that trip alone in an automobile.

Herb Colmer

Hauling lumber at the mill. Nelson farm in background.

Nelson's Store
Aug. 3, 1916

C/O B.F. Barnett, Franklin, Ind.
Brother,

Hope you & family are haveing a fine time at the Barnett Reunion. Well I believe you are right the timber prospects for next winter are pitiful all the good wood is gone. Took dinner with Elmer and Elise LeVesseur at Pine Beach and they think same. Elmer still has that fine big team of Nig and Prince. He says if you decide to run a camp up his way again next winter do not fail to sign him on.

Injuns have taken to calling him "Man with the Big Team." Joe Cayo is "Sawmill Man," Mrs. Cayo "Wife of Sawmill Man." Elise is "Wife of Man with Big Team." I cant say how it sounds in Chippewa.

Fred

Elmer LeVesseur.

Pine Beach, Sandy Lake
Aug 9 16

Mr. Nelson -

Mrs. Larson got after me on account her fresh meat was bad when I unloaded it. They live so far out in the woods if a box of rocks was sent up, they'd spoil before half way there.

If O.K. with you, on the grocery runs I will rig up an ice box to fit into my wagon and fill at Lang's ice house at the drive camp.

Elmer LeVesseur

Trafalgar, Ind.
11-14-16

Cousin Myrtle,

You say your Ma read my last letter. Oh my. What all did she say? How has Gust O. been treating you lately? Is he still your protector? Did you give him that X I sent him?

We shall have an Algebra Exam Thursday morning. I pity myself.

Why don't that little brat of an Orvis answer my letter?

What kind of English books do you study? We are studying Eliot's "Silas Marner." It is interesting. We shall soon be ready to study Caesar. It is the hardest on account it's nothing stuff I know of.

I will end with this:

"Long may you live, happy may you die -
Sitting on the wood pile, eating pumpkin pie.

"Crackers are good but cheese is better-
If you love me, answer this letter. (Soon.)

"Turn your shoes toward the street,
leave your garters on your feet -
Tie your stockings 'round your head,
and dream of the man you're going to wed.

"When I am dead and in my grave,
and all my bones are rotten -
This little note will tell my name,
when I am quite forgotten.

"I write not for fortune,
I write not for fame -
I write to be remembered,
and here I sign my name.
Miss Elfel Barnett

Nelson Pony Farm
Dec 11 of 1916

Maddy Hotel, McGregor
To Papa from Bud,

Yesterday after church we went on a skating party to Duglas Lake. Took Sleights out and sang songs. We had a big fire in the middle of the lake and when it got dark we could still see. Esther Steffer cut backward circles in the ice then we played crack the whip & I was on the end. O Boy! Ernest skated too close to the Island and busted through but it was onley up to his knees. We ate a big Oyster supper and then it was time to come home. I think I fell asleep in the hay wagon.

Did you find a Indian birch bark canoe for my Xmas present?

Your son

Waubun, Minn.
1/30/17

Marcus,

I suppose you thought the old boy has croaked. Don't you believe it. I have been trying to see how much work I could do the first month in the year.

I want the bees to work to beat Old Nick this coming season, and make enough extra so that I can go South next winter. This is the coldest place in winter that I ever saw. It seems to get colder proportional to the number of years I spend on this old earth. Well, no more of that for old Jay if I can help it, thank you.

We have got plenty of freezing wind but not much snow and the plowed fields are bare in places. Makes it look bleak as (well just bleak).

I have been in town but once this winter and I'm not going again until it gets warmer. If I can get time will have a look at Tamarack when it greens up.

JBC

Nelson Pony Farm
Sunday, Feb 18, 17

My Dear Miss Myrtle Paxson,

It is your turn to come over here as my Myrtle was out to your place yesterday. It's kind of cool this morning, just what you'd notice.

You ought to have seen me coming down the lane yesterday. Babe ran off with me. She went some, believe me. I ran her in deep snow so she had to stop. Old Hector barked and frightened her.

Beloved Babe.

Well I am sorry I missed the Valentine Party, but I did not know if us old ladies was wanted or not. I am coming soon to visit the school and I will see you there.

Did Myrtle tell you she found a little mouse froze last week? Look inside for a picture I drew of her doll house.

Your loving friend, Mamie Nelson

Nelson Pony Farm
April 9, 1917

Dear Dumb Myrtle -
    Didja ever think as time went by
        that you might be the next to die?
    They dig a hole six feet deep
        and stuff you in a big white sheet.
    The worms crawl in the worms crawl out
        the worms play pea nuckle on your snout.
    Your body turns to a slimey green
        an pus comes out like whipping cream.
    And Myrtle without a spoon!
        HA!   HA!   HA!   HA!   HA!
    Yours, etc.
    Orvis Marcus Nelson

Nelson Pony Farm
May 23, '17

C/O Tingdale Bros., Mpls
Husband,
    The children went on revolt as soon as you left this morning. They begun the fight by refusing to take their castor oil and when I put my foot down they ran out of the house without finishing breakfast.
    Are a handful as usual when you are gone. You do not see or choose not to see what kind of trouble I have with them because you are too soft to punish when you get home & they know it.
    If that were not enough, Orvis stabbed Norton Kelley in the foot this forenoon. They were playing mumblety-peg and Orvis got too stretched out and was off balance when he threw the knife. I washed, painted, and bandaged the wound do not think stitching was needed. The boy took it well but limped home.
    Finish your work and come home do not go off over the weekend to another of those vaudeville shows, that stuff is a scandal.
    Mamie
P.S. If you do not approve of the way I explain the birds & bees to Myrtle you are welcome to give it a try yourself.

Tamarack Post Office
July 17 - 17

Mr. Nelson:
    Wish to advise that Rural Free Delivery (RFD) & Star Route contract delivery has at last been approved for our district. Mr. Koplen and Mr. Kelley will share carrier duties. We expect from this change to provide more efficient mail service to the outlying areas of the community.
    J. Mayhall, Postmaster

Nelson Pony Farm
Sept 6, '17

Curtiss Hotel, Mpls
Husband,
    Orvis cannot control himself when you are away. He and a Beggs boy were up above the north field playing along the tracks, hopping freights to and from town, no matter the many times I have told him not to do such fool things. On the last round, they jumped off near the Comfort Hotel and Orvis fell into Sicottis' old well. Like to have gone straight to the bottom and drowned but for an old timber he clung to till help arrived. Have the town to lose a child for that well to be filled in once and for all? Gave him a talking to but do not know if it did any good.
    Mr. Carr has been busy with barn chores and fixing machinery. He found a girl for me to help with all the work around the house. This afternoon we finished putting up 400 jars of fruit, also canned corn on the cob as we are all so fond of it.
    Mamie

Nelson Pony Farm
9:30 PM, 12-12-17

Husband,

We had an adventure today. Cliff Martin, Ken & Gerald Beggs, Floyd Cyrus, and Orvis were released from school and sent out on a Christmas tree hunt. I did not know they would be going or would have objected as it was 30 below at noon.

They followed the dredge ditch south to Spruce Lake as had determined they wanted a spruce instead of balsam as spruce does not burn as easily. Cliff Martin had a revolver along and shot them a couple of rabbits & they built a lean-to and roasted the game. After filling up, the boys chopped down a nice spruce and cut off the top fifteen feet of it. Ken Beggs said would take the first turn so the rest of them went on ahead and tramped snow while Ken dragged the tree top behind.

About this time the boys spotted a deer and, showing as much sense as a sled dog, forgot their job and lit out after it. When finally they tired of the chase came back looking for Ken but no Ken. One of the boys heard hollering, found he had broke thru the ice & was thrashing around in open water. They calmed him down, pushed the tree out, and drug him in. He was turning into a blue icicle so they built a fire, rigged a windbreak, and stripped off his clothes. Each boy gave up a layer & Ken had dry clothes again.

Was 5 o'clock & pitch dark when they came dragging the tree up to school. Orvis said Miss Tool was agitated and ready to sound alarm, but boys told her everything was fine and said nothing of what happened. I only got the full report out of our son an hour ago.

Mamie

P.S. I just got up to look and my thermometer says it is over 50 below.

From left, Orvis, Cliff, Gerald, & Ken.

Tamarack School District #53
Friday, December 21st, 1917

OUR BRAVE LITTLE TREE
Our brave and sturdy little tree
    was growing in the wood
It stood as straight as straight could be
    as every brave tree should
It bore not juicy apples
    nor cherries red and round
It never dropped bright autumn leaves
    beneath it on the ground

But its arms were open wide
    to catch the breezes bold
It sang a cheery little song
    And did not mind the cold

When other trees were sleeping
    as bare as bare could be
Our little tree was bright and gay
    for it was evergreen

Oh! Then its heart was happy
    the children's joy to see
As they danced and cried in gladness
    Oh! What a lovely tree!

END NOTES

Part One

Special Notes: "The Ancient Trail," a charcoal sketch by Mamie B. Nelson appearing on the covers, portrays a centuries old Indian trail that followed the south bank of the Prairie River to where it entered Sandy Lake. Construction of a new bridge and road in 1958, coupled with the accelerated erosion this work triggered, has completely destroyed the trail. Also, because Mamie Barnett had not yet arrived on the scene, all the letters appearing in Part One were derived from family histories and other secondary sources.

10/10/92, O. Nielsen: Big game was largely taken in the fall, so the meat could be kept frozen until ready for use.

6/10/93, Fred Nielsen: Local lore insists a section of one of those big pines was sent to the Columbian Exposition in Chicago.

7/6/93, Emma Friestad: Due to lack of money and so many mouths to feed at Nielsen Lake, Hans Friestad was away to the Twin Cities practicing his tailor trade for much of 1893-1898.

12/25/94, Josie Nielsen: Helga Friestad was the first full-blood white child born in what became Clark Township.

4/15/95, Ben Gunderson: Tom Hull's hunting accident actually happened to an unidentified settler a few years later.

9/3/95, F. Nielsen: After the Indians harvested the wild rice, they placed it in pots over a low fire to cook (parch). To loosen the hulls, they "danced" (trampled) on the grain. To remove the chaff, the rice was placed on birch trays and, with a side-arm motion, the hulls were fanned away.

11/16/95, B. Gunderson: This was before laws against commercial harvesting of fish and wildlife were enacted and enforced.

3/13/96, F. Nielsen: Years later, Marcus told Orvis he did not believe Ben's death was accidental.

4/15/96, Jay Clark: Today, carnelians are more commonly called agates, a semi-precious stone. "Panthers," or mountain lions, were not uncommon in the region at that time. Interestingly, there have been recent unconfirmed sightings of lions in Aitkin and Carlton counties.

6/15/96, O. Nielsen: Most people were confused by the monetary issues of the day. Bryan advocated a return to using silver coinage as well as gold (at a ratio of 16 ounces of silver equal to one ounce of gold). He believed a more liberal, "free silver," policy would improve the lives of the common man by increasing the amount of cash in circulation (times had been hard in the early '90s). McKinley stood with the bankers and the exclusive gold standard. Gold won out at the time, but history suggests Bryan was right.

7/19/96, J. Clark: A tip of the hat for the "rock telegraph" story to Mr. Ed Barrow, "Aitkin County Heritage," page 59 (bibliography).

5/18/97, Josie: A timber cruiser estimated the value of marketable timber on a tract of land and mapped it out for logging.

6/23/97, O. Nielsen: It was long believed that trees grew where the ground was most fertile. "Skinning the logs" refers to walking over a "bridge" of logs laid end to end over swampy ground.

8/28/97, F. Nielsen: Traveling by way of "shanks mare" meant walking.

11/14/98, F. Nelson: On October 6-8, 1898, the so-called "Battle of Sugar Lake" occurred at Leech Lake, Minnesota. Historians consider this relatively minor skirmish the last organized conflict between Indian forces and the U.S. Army. It's probable that incident sparked the fiasco at McGregor. A similar "massacre" took place in the Aitkin area about the same time.

5/17/99, O. Nielsen: The Nielsen farm (excepting the house) was destroyed in the 1894 Hinckley Fire and then the house itself burned down around the turn of the century. It was the last straw for Niels Nielsen, but it wasn't the end for this star-crossed homestead. Dennis Carr would be burned out of this same farm in 1918!

7/5/99, O. Nielsen: This letter is based on a Barott family account, given to Mamie Nelson for her 1958 History of Tamarack.

Part Two

9/10/00, Mamie: Chippewa, Ojibwe, Ojibwa, and Ojibway all refer to the same Algonquian group of Native Americans. Out loud, rapidly repeat the word O-jib-wah and listen how it can turn into Chippewa. A Victorian woman wearing breeches (trousers) was somewhat scandalous.

9/17/00, J. Cayo: In 1958, Arthur Heath gave a graphic account of the early "roads": "[When we first came to Tamarack] the road out [to Balsam Township] was terrific . . . The going was rough and Mother had a hard time staying in the wagon, to say nothing of trying to enjoy the scenery . . . After she got out there, it was a couple of years before she went to town again."

5/12/01, M. Tingdale: I wrote the majority of the Martin Tingdale and all of the Ed Douglas letters, but they are not invention; their function is to provide accurate narration and maintain story cohesiveness.

7/24/02, M. Barnett: M.E. stood for Methodist Episcopal. Protracted meetings (revivals) might be held for three or four weeks at a time, and were half entertainment, half evangelical in nature.

3/30/03, Pat Barott: This letter is drawn from an account by Barry LeVesseur, Alfred Barott's grandson. "Jinsing", or ginseng, was a rare and wild cash crop in demand as a substitute for opium and as a medicine, especially in China.

5/2/06, Emma Friestad: The accompanying photo is actually the Odegard School two miles north of Tamarack, circa 1905-10.

7/13/06, Mamie: The Chautauqua (named after the first one near Lake Chautauqua, N.Y.) was a very popular form of inspirational entertainment until radio stamped it out. This experience may or may not have actually happened.

12/10/06, Ida Crandall: "Fish ponds" were fund raising gimmicks. You paid for a 5 or 10 cent "line" and dangled your "pole" over the back of a booth, where someone tied on a prize.

3/19/07, Emma: Apparently a traveling salesman called Orvis passed through and both Mamie & Marcus liked the name.

4/25/08, Clark: At the time, Detroit Lakes, Minnesota was known as "Detroit" or "Detroit City."

6/11/08, Douglas: The bronc busting episode is based on an account in Orvis' 1942 unpublished autobiography (bibliography), and is true except that Marcus was at the corral and played out the role I assigned to Douglas. Also, Mamie's cash winnings may have been $75.00 in paper money rather than the $20 gold piece. And yes, his name really was E.Z. Mark!

3/30/09, Maggie Nay: Tin marks a Tenth Wedding Anniversary, china a Twentieth.

8/3/09, Mamie: City people have breakfast, lunch, and dinner - with occasional daytime and evening snacks. Many rural Minnesota communities to this day have breakfast, dinner, and supper - with mid-morning, mid-afternoon, and evening lunches.

11/15/09, Mamie: In a 1958 letter to Mamie, Gust Oja wrote that "one day in 1908 [I went] to Tamarack to buy me a pair of shoes. I can still remember the wonderful smells when I stepped into that store. All the pretty things for sale awed me and the candy and oranges were out of this world. I hoped someday I could live in town and I would buy all I wanted. I got a pair of pretty high topped shoes, the first store shoes I ever had. Then the man in the store said something to me I did not understand. He took me by the arm behind the counter and pointed to the candy. I was drooling alright but I had no money so I had to shake my head. He took a large candy bag and filled it with assorted candies, led me back to the door and told me good by and something else I could not understand. I thought he was the most wonderful man in the world, which he proved to me many times later on. That man was Marcus Nelson."

8/11/11, Mamie: There were also yellow, blue & red diamond trails (primitive roads). The colored diamond shaped markers were hung or painted on trees, posts, etc. They were easy to miss, especially at night.

5/10/12, Myrtle's story: This is her version of an Aesop Fable.

5/14/12, Mamie: It was all the rage early in the century to make personalized photo post cards.

10/2/12, Mamie: My Dad and I discovered Topsy's heavy concrete marker in 1956 when we were landscaping a new yard. In 1996, after researching Topsy's "funeral" for this book, I re-discovered the marker buried under a pile of old ties! This time I and my faithful Allis-Chalmers WD tractor put it in a safe place. The photo Mamie made accompanying the "gypsy" reference is something of a mystery. There were all manner of transients along a transcontinental railroad.

3/26/13, Mamie: It is hard to believe that Tamarack did not get rid of it's crank phones until 1958, when dial service was extended from McGregor. At that time, our farm's ring was one long and two short. For a long distance call, you had to place or take it at cousin Helga Friestad's central office. By this time, Orvis Nelson, an aviation pioneer whose story we will examine in detail in a later volume, had founded Transocean Air Lines. The clumsy telephone arrangement was a source of great amusement at the airline's headquarters in Oakland, California whenever they were trying to track down their President. I can still see Helga running down Main Street, yelling at the top of her lungs in the direction of our store, "Orvis! Orvis! Long distance!" Helga's original switchboard, chair, and telephone logs can be viewed at the Aitkin County Historical Society's Depot Museum in downtown Aitkin, Minnesota.

6/13/15, Lang: During the first half of the 19th century, a final series of battles was fought on Battle Island between the Lakota (Sioux) and the Ojibway (Chippewa) for control of the region. Due to superior armament (gotten from the white man), the latter won out.

4/9/17, Orvis: This children's ditty was still floating around Tamarack when I was a boy.

5/23/17, Mamie: While I invented this mumblety-peg incident, I have no doubt the boys played the game.

7/17/17, J. Mayhall: Star Routes were mail routes contracted out by the federal government to a person or firm. The days of sporadic mail delivery by a backpacking carrier were over.

12/12/17, Mamie: This is the way Orvis related the Christmas tree adventure in his 1942 autobiography. I am fairly certain this incident happened in December, 1917.

12/21/17, Tamarack School: The brave little tree poem appeared in Myrtle's school notebook.

PHOTO AND ILLUSTRATION CREDITS

- The three front cover photos (which also appear on pages M, 21 and 38 are by Mamie B. Nelson. Also appearing on the covers is "The Ancient Trail," a charcoal sketch by Mamie B. Nelson.
- Title pages B and C, Nielsen homestead, photo by Mamie B. Nelson (M.B.N.).
- F, 1820 Schoolcraft map, by Henry Schoolcraft.
- G, Regional map, by Aitkin Independent Age.
- H, Nielsen 1880 family photo, Grimstad, Norway. Studio Portrait.
- I, Niels Nielsen carving figureheads, Grimstad studio portrait circa 1870s.
- I, J and K, Smith-Petersen Boatworks and sea side and landside images of Grimstad fjord are from the 1927 edition of *Grimstad Bys Historie*, by permission and courtesy of the Ibsenhuset and Grimstad Bymuseum, Grimstad, Norway. The two letters of recommendation appearing on these pages were transcribed from the originals by John Kaldahl, Emma Friestad's grandson.
- L, Drawing of Sicottis' Trading Post, by M.B.N.
- 1, Mr. and Mrs. Ole Nielsen, Minnesota studio portrait.
- 1, Marcus Nielsen and Jay Clark, studio portrait.
- 1, Fred Nielsen, studio portrait.
- 2, Declaration of Intention, M.B.N. letter collection.
- 3, Dick Reed, by M.B.N.
- 4, Nielsens and Friestads at homestead, by M.B.N.
- 6, Virgin pine, probably by Orvis M. Nelson.
- 6, Emma Friestad, studio portrait.
- 7, Josephine Nielsen, studio portrait.
- 8, Charcoal sketch of men in canoe, by M.B.N.
- 9, Locomotive and car, Aitkin County Historical Society collection (A.C.H.S.)
- 9, Deer on platform, by M.B.N.
- 11, ..."built their campfires...," by M.B.N.
- 11, Mississippi River, A.C.H.S. collection.
- 12, N.P. section crew, A.C.H.S. collection.
- 13, Two Grass Twine Co. photos, A.C.H.S. collection.
- 14, Friestad family, probably by M.B.N.
- 15, Certificate of Citizenship, M.B.N. letter collection.
- 16, Maple sugaring, A.C.H.S. collection.

- 20, 1896 portrait of Barnett children, et.al., Barnett family photo.
- 20, Mamie at eighteen, Indiana studio portrait.
- 22, Drawing of Sicottis Station, by M.B.N.
- 23 and 24, Four photos of "old store," by M.B.N.
- 25, Lilliedales, studio portrait.
- 25, Misses Forsythe and Anderson, by M.B.N.
- 26, Mamie Barnett, studio portrait.
- 26, Tote road, by M.B.N.
- 27, Marcus on chair, by M.B.N.
- 27, B.F. & M.E. Barnett, studio portraits.
- 28, Wedding picture, Duluth studio portrait.
- 28, Methodist church, commercial post card.
- 29, Stove drawing, by M.B.N.
- 30, Myrtle Barnett, studio portrait.
- 32, Barnett home painting, artist unknown.
- 32, Frank Barnett, family photo.
- 33, Baby Myrtle, by M.B.N.
- 33, 1904 envelope, M.B.N. letter collection.
- 34, Unidentified settlers, by M.B.N.
- 36, School house, photographer unknown.
- 37, Minnehaha Falls, commercial postcard.
- 37, Mamie and baby Myrtle, composed by M.B.N.
- 38, Aitkin County church, A.C.H.S. collection.
- 39, Fred Nelson children, by M.B.N.
- 39, Orvis and friends, by M.B.N.
- 40, Round Lake, by M.B.N.
- 42, Three Round Lake camping photos, by M.B.N.
- 43, Newstrom livery, A.C.H.S. collection.
- 43, Tamarack corral, by M.B.N.
- 44, Sand bar, by M.B.N.
- 45, Home place, composed by M.B.N.
- 46, Family montage, composed by M.B.N.
- 47, Barn, by M.B.N.
- 48, Gust Oja, probably by M.B.N.
- 48, Stationary letterhead, M.B.N. letter collection.
- 49, Bathing beauties, composed by M.B.N.
- 50, Friestad's, probably by M.B.N.
- 51, Children in cart, by M.B.N.
- 51, Ponies at house, composed by M.B.N.
- 52, Nelson family, studio portrait.
- 53, Sleigh, composed by M.B.N.
- 53, Saddle mare, family post card.
- 54, Card to "Bud," commercial post card.
- 55, The race, by M.B.N.
- 55, Carr and cats, by M.B.N.
- 56, Topsy, by M.B.N.

- 56, Transients near depot, by M.B.N.
- 57, Two 4th of July photos, probably by M.B.N.
- 58, Ferry crossing, A.C.H.S. collection.
- 58, Original Prairie River Bridge, probably
    by Orvis M. Nelson.
- 58, Tamarack School, probably by M.B.N.
- 59, Daisy's play, photographer unknown.
- 60, Myrtle's report card, M.B.N. letter collection.
- 61, Loading hay, by M.B.N.
- 62, Woman in boat, probably by M.B.N.
- 63, Tamarack lumber yard, probably by M.B.N.
- 64, Elmer LeVesseur, probably by M.B.N.
- 65, Babe, composed by M.B.N.
- 67, Schoolboys, probably by Ella Tool, teacher.
- 68, Xmas tree, commercial post card.
- The map on page G was prepared in part by the
    Aitkin County Land Department, GIS
    Division. Aitkin County does not assume
    any liability for errors, omissions or
    inaccuracies herein contained.

BIBLIOGRAPHY

- *Aitkin Age, 1892-1912*, weekly newspaper, St. Paul: Minnesota Historical Society microfilm files.
- *Aitkin Independent, 1901-1912*, weekly newspaper, St. Paul: Minnesota Historical Society microfilm files.
- *Aitkin Independent Age, 1912-1938*, weekly newspaper, St. Paul: Minnesota Historical Society microfilm files.
- *Aitkin Republican, 1894-1938*, weekly newspaper, St. Paul: Minnesota Historical Society microfilm files.
- *Aitkin 1871-1971: The Centennial Story of a Town*, Aitkin, Minnesota: Aitkin Area Centennial Executive Committee, 1971.
- Allen, Frederick Lewis, *The Big Change: America Transforms Itself 1900 - 1950*, New York: Harper & Brothers, 1952.
- Barnett, Mary A., *History of the Barnett Family*, Indianapolis, Indiana: Self published, 1923 (revised 1977).
- Botkin, B.A., Editor, *A Treasury of American Folklore*, New York: Crown Publishers, 1944.
- Cram, George, F. Publisher, *Cram's Unrivaled Family Atlas of the World*, Chicago & New York, 1900.
- Cross, Marion E., *Pioneer Harvest*, Minneapolis, Minnesota: The Farmers and Mechanics Savings Bank of Minneapolis, 1949.
- Cyrus, Erline Kelley, *taped interview*, 1994
- Editors of American Heritage, *The Confident Years*, New York: American Heritage Publishing Co. Inc., No date.

- Folwell, William Watts, *A History of Minnesota*, 4 volumes, Saint Paul: Minnesota Historical Society, 1921, 1924, 1926, 1930.
- *Gehring Hotel Directory and Tourist Guide*, New York: Gehring Publishing Company, October, 1926.
- Kaldahl, John, *The Nielsens and the Friestads — Norwegian Families Homestead in Minnesota*, Alexandria, Virginia: Self published, 1981.
- Kent, Kai Kelley, Editor, *Among the Tamaracks*, Tamarack, Minnesota: Self published, no date (circa 1980).
- Nelson, Mamie, *Pioneer History of Tamarack*, unpublished, 109 typewritten pages, 1958.
- Nelson, Marcus & Mamie, *family and business letter collection*, 1901-1939.
- Nelson, Mamie, *photograph and illustration collection*.
- Nelson, Orvis M., *unpublished autobiography*, 441 typewritten pages, 1942.
- Rosenberg, S.H., Editor, *Rural America: A Century Ago*, St. Joseph, Michigan: American Society of Agricultural Engineers, 1976.
- Written by the People of Aitkin County, *Aitkin County Heritage*, Aitkin, Minnesota: Aitkin County Historical Society, 1991.
- Wyman, Walker (with Kurt Leichtle), *The Chippewa: A History of the Great Lakes Woodland Tribe over Three Centuries*, River Falls, Wisconsin: University of Wisconsin - River Falls Press, 1993.

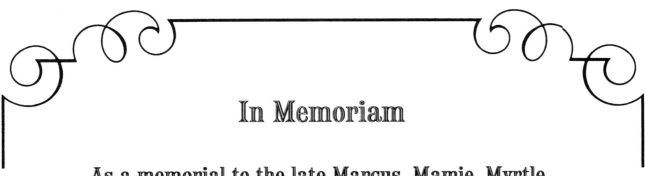

In Memoriam

As a memorial to the late Marcus, Mamie, Myrtle,
and Orvis Nelson, we, their extended family,

Robert H. Harder, Myrtle's husband,
and Robert O. and Carol, their children

Edith F. Nelson, Orvis' wife,
and Holly, Sue, Marcus, and Jeffrey,
their children

are pleased to donate all of the net profits earned
from the sale of this book to the
Aitkin County Historical Society.

The Aitkin County Historical Society Press (ACHSP) is proud to announce a new title to our line of published books – *A Minnesota Remembrance: Making a Life in the Land God Forgot* by Robert O. Harder.

The Aitkin County Historical Society is a nonprofit local history society that offers a research facility for family genealogy and local history, and an historical object collection. The society's collection is housed in two facilities, a 1950 log structure that was the first museum building in Aitkin County and a 1916 Northern Pacific Railway depot building.

The society's mission is to collect, preserve and disseminate knowledge of Aitkin County heritage. ACHSP would like to thank the Harder and Nelson families for their generous contribution of this book to the historical society. Projects such as this enable the society to continue the mission of preserving our past for future generations.

The Aitkin County Historical Society museum buildings and office are located in downtown Aitkin, Minnesota. When visiting the museum don't forget to stop and browse in our book and gift shop in the Depot Museum.

~ Jerry Rosnau
Director